Frugal

Living

Easy Ways to Spend Less and Save More

(Step by Step Guide to a Frugal Life With Financial Freedom)

Daniel McKinney

Published By **Bengion Cosalas**

Daniel McKinney

Frugal Living: Easy Ways to Spend Less and Save More (Step by Step Guide to a Frugal Life With Financial Freedom)

ISBN 978-1-7770981-7-9

No part of this guidebook shall be reproduced in any form without permission in writing from the publisher except in the case of brief quotations embodied in critical articles or reviews.

Legal & Disclaimer

The information contained in this book is not designed to replace or take the place of any form of medicine or professional medical advice. The information in this book has been provided for educational & entertainment purposes only.

The information contained in this book has been compiled from sources deemed reliable, and it is accurate to the best of the Author's knowledge; however, the Author cannot guarantee its accuracy and validity and cannot be held liable for any errors or omissions. Changes are periodically made to this book. You must consult your doctor or get professional medical advice before using any of the suggested remedies, techniques, or information in this book.

Table Of Contents

Chapter 1: Housing

Housing easily expenses maximum of our profits, so permit's start there. This version is for the proprietors, so permit's see how we're capable of shop cash at the houses we private (mortgaged or paid off).

Refinance

Interest fees at the time of this writing are significantly low. That is why we refinanced our home after a trifling two years of living here. We offered at a time the marketplace seemed bullish and we had been afraid that the hobby prices could in all likelihood skyrocket.

Let's simply prevent right right right here: it is highly difficult to play the marketplace.

If we did it right, we might have presented one of the houses we had been looking at once more in 2012. Home charges have been still rock backside due to the housing bubble. However, we couldn't find out "the proper one" with our constrained finances and needed to wait some other six years. Don't think we didn't look at houses subsequently of that factor. We have been continuously at the hunt for the proper house. To the issue that it became inflicting scientific despair.

We manifestly didn't play the market. People will assist you to understand to shop for at the same time as costs are low, however I will permit you to recognize this: purchase whilst you want a domestic. If you believe you studied the charges are too excessive and choice for another market bust, you may take a seat and watch expenses climb like they've got in the previous few years (scripting this to you in 2022).

Truth be instructed, no character in truth is aware of how matters are going to play out. If you need a home and characteristic the approach to shop for one, don't allow any "what if" get within the manner.

We at the begin had been given an hobby price of four.25%. Still low from a historic point of view, but at the identical time as hobby expenses nonetheless decreased, in assessment to marketplace predictions cautioned me they could, we ended up refinancing at 2.625%.

Didn't you need to pay each different down charge? Yes, but the quantity of coins we'll preserve in the long run made it properly honestly really worth it. Plus, the down rate come to be absorbed into the loan. We didn't want to shell out any cash from the bed or some thing.

Husband: Check out NerdWallet to perform a little math and be aware if it is truly well worth it to refinance. They are going to ask you precise questions about your cutting-edge-day-day and possible mortgage, so have the ones accessible if feasible! With refinancing there are basically options relying on the maturity of the loan (how a long way through the whole mortgage are you)? You should attempt and reduce your month-to-month rate to transport away room for those better interest loans you could have or try and shorten the time of the mortgage. We were able to transfer from a 30-year loan to a 20-three hundred and sixty five days whilst basically retaining the monthly rate the equal. The elegant quantity we're able to preserve genuinely amazed me! Since interest costs change during the 365 days, take a look at from time to time to look if it is honestly without a doubt worth it for you. Too busy to do this? Well, NerdWallet will watch the hobby fees (and likely deliver you a few inbox fillers right here and there) and notify you even as it is probably worth it as a way to refinance!

Utilities

Next up at the listing of payments to lessen: Utilities (yeah, the ones subjects ain't appealing however you don't need to be bow-chicka-wow-wow-ing with the intention to keep coins).

Change filters

You spend tough-earned cash cooling your air. What can get inside the manner of the flow of your hard-earned cool air? Your dirt! Yea, it's far absolutely disgusting. But regularly converting your filters does extra for you than simply improving your air quality. How? Because you aren't doling out extra cash to electrically push the air through the funk.

Find normal intervals at a few degree within the one year and peg the activity of changing them to it so that you don't overlook. Maybe the number one day of every season? Like a ritual that addiction stacks converting air filters and some component else you like to do frequently.

I love rituals. They make existence more considerable.

For instance, we eat one caramel apple a 12 months. Why? Because it's too highly-priced to buy one every and each time we see the carnival laid out within the mall car parking zone. So, we purchase a % of caramel apples on fall solstice to have fun the season of spooky and pumpkin spice.

That'd be a outstanding day to recall to exchange the filter. Caramel apples and easy dwelling. Money stored in the course of the three hundred and sixty five days. Now you truly want another issue to have amusing each of the three other seasons.

Husband: How regularly you need to exchange your filter out may also moreover rely upon your living conditions. Living with cats/puppies/different bushy pets? You'll likely want to exchange them out earlier than otherwise. They make filters in some thicknesses and with remarkable attributes. Some filters block out lint, household dust, and pollen at the identical time as others can block out mould spores, pup dander, or even bacteria in a few instances! Consumer Reports has a terrific article on air filters.

Change your mild bulbs

You realise the trunk of slight bulbs you inherited from your great aunt because she changed into a incredible melancholy survivor who hoarded out of comfort? Throw those out! Unless they're collectibles (is that a problem??)

Outdated light bulbs may be costing you coins. Too a good deal electricity is transformed to heat as opposed to mild. Therefore, costing you each to moderate the room, however moreover cool it go into reverse from the extra warm temperature for the duration of the summertime. Upgrade your bulbs at once and start saving nowadays.

Chapter 2: Cold water, whenever

If you ever see me with out my kids, you've caught me in the tub. That is my sanctuary. Unless it's miles the sea, there may be no water better than sore-muscle-soaking warmness water.

I love warmness baths! So an entire lot so that I truly much like the concept of warmth water. When I visit wash my hands, I instinctively turn the present day water deal with like I'm balloting for my favourite American Idol. I simply determine on warmness water to cold water. But most of the time, it takes a while for the brand new water from the closet under the stairs to attain my hands on the kitchen sink.

The warmness water starts where it grow to be born: the new water heater. Of path, we realise water isn't born within the warm water heater, but its hotness became born there (till you stay in Arizona

- then the brand new water exists simply with the resource of way of being H_2O molecules inside the silliest place to stay in America (I'm no matter the truth that seeking to get my outstanding friend all of the time to move to my u . S . A . As opposed to her silly u . S .)). It then keeps its adventure via a length of pipes. The period relies upon on how far away your tap is from your heat water heater. This journey takes time. Most of the time, it takes longer than the 20 seconds it is advocated to scrub your fingers.

So the recent water faucet is grew to come to be go into reverse earlier than the heated water even makes it to my fingers. Now, does that imply no longer something befell with the current water? No! It began out its journey. The high-priced heat water made its manner to the tap, however I completed earlier than it can get there and have become the faucet off. Trapping the volume of warm water somewhere under my house, forgotten and lonely.

We pay for that warm temperature.

And then we allow it waste. The warmth now sits under our flooring, needlessly heating the pipes and dissipating heat we don't word (however our cooling invoice notices it - at the least a piece). Then the current water heater has to churn up over again to top off the little bit of water wasted. All because of our "choice" for respectable water.

Wash your palms with cold water. Every time. It makes no feel to warmth the pipes for no motive.

This may not look like hundreds, but bear in mind each time you wash your fingers, more than one instances an afternoon.

Unless your warm water can excursion to the tap at an inexpensive tempo, really use bloodless water.

Lower water temperature

This one pains me to speak about because of the fact my preferred interest is pretty an entire lot scalding myself within the bathtub. But it is a large cash saver. Therefore, I want to include it: decrease the temperature on your water heater.

According the energy.Gov, "for each 10ºF bargain in temperature, you can keep from three%–five% for your water heating prices." yay.

It moreover reduces the hazard of a person getting harm. Little kids within the bath can all too with out issue obtain over and run the new water proper on their pores and pores and skin, resulting in severe harm. And sure, lowering the temperature will shop coins at the medical payments, however I think saving them from 0.33 diploma burns takes priority over saving coins in this situation (fine example of ways you might imagine too cheap). Safety over the whole thing!

Only run domestic gadget complete

On your washing gadget you'll see a knob that gives you the selection of load length (or a button that sings like a canary whilst you press it for you fancy mother and father). Small, medium, or large. Only keep it on massive and best turn it on if it's far virtually a huge load.

It makes no feel to fill the tank half of-complete. You get no reduce fee on strength. Yes, you'll use a good deal much less water, however the system however runs. It makes no revel in.

The identical detail goes for the dishwasher. Never run it besides the weight is whole.

But I want only a few subjects washed in advance than our subsequent meal. Then wash them thru hand. While considering your heated water consumption, of path.

But what approximately the dryer? Only run it at some stage in wintry climate. Well, how am I supposed to take care of my laundry? Let the solar do it! More on that later. Yeah, we're going all Little House on The Prairie in this residence!

Unplug what is no longer in use

Take a go searching the room you're in. Can you spot the hollow? How many stuff are plugged in? Now, how quite a few those matters plugged in are presently in use? If they're have emerge as off, they aren't the usage of strength, proper?

Wrong! They are draining power. Granted, it cannot be an entire lot, but with all the rooms and all the plugs and all of the appliances, that provides up to masses of energy. As an awful lot as $2 hundred in the commonplace domestic!

So, you're pronouncing I ought to unplug everything while it's not in use? Yep! Even worrying plugs which can be hard to obtain similar to the tv or laptop? Yeah, this is stressful. Maybe choose out a electricity surge protector issue that you can turn a switch to close down. Or truly unplug in a single fell swoop.

There's no actual cause to have them plugged in while now not in use. You comprehend me with the resource of manner of now, I must deliver in a favorite stand up bit and I'll depart it to the King of Comedy (at least to me), Mitch Hedberg to provide an cause of this one:

"I don't have a microwave oven, but I do have a clock that every so often cooks stuff."

How frequently do you operate your microwave? Once a day? A couple of times a day? Either manner, you could effortlessly create the dependancy of unplugging it after use. Clean and decorate your counters in the sort of way that it is an clean venture. After all, you don't need a clock inside the kitchen besides. You have your cell telephone. Or, better however, mount one at the wall so that you do now not by way of the usage of twist of fate get sucked into the social media scroll honestly because of the truth you needed to check the time (or am I the best one?)

The 2nd manner unplugging what's no longer in use saves cash is due to power surges. Think approximately your lighting when you turn at the dryer. Or the vacuum. Or the hairdryer. It's like ghosts flickering lights at the sound of your chores, even for best a quick second. Those are electricity surges.

If you have were given an gadget plugged in and each different one roars up, causing that electricity surge, all plugged in home system take a hit. This decreases the longevity of these domestic system. Just such as you don't want to be shopping for the cutting-edge-day vibrant tool definitely due to the reality, you don't want to be changing those you've got were given just because of the reality you're too lazy to take the 10 seconds to unplug it, ultimately saving the equal of a month's energy bill.

Chapter 3: Check out home performance programs

Our vicinity's strength companies offer a application where they arrive to your house and improve many electricity saving objects freed from charge. For instance, a collection of guys got here to our residence and grew to emerge as it into the ET medical scene. They wrapped the home windows and doors in plastic and blew a big fan, tracking some device that examine how inexperienced our domestic grow to be at maintaining drafts. It felt so sci-fi. It have become a touch overwhelming taking walks with a little one on my hip via my home cosplaying like against the law scene.

This software program application had the organization come and replace all of our mild bulbs with electricity green ones. They even may additionally've insulated our domestic if it favored it.

Check spherical your location to appearance if there are each other comparable home efficiency applications. It need to prevent masses.

If there aren't, make certain to do all the topics they did for me besides. Insulating your attic and basement must save you round $two hundred in step with 12 months. Definitely properly really well worth the funding.

Bake multiple things straight away

There isn't always a whole lot better than the go with the flow of appropriate cooking from the oven rolling via the house. I'm speakme about home made bread or chocolate chip cookies to have an outstanding time that time of the month (for the ones humans who have a few slip-u.S. Of americain bed, you apprehend once in a while Aunt Flo merits a few celebrating).

However, one manner of saving coins is difficult those smells thru manner of baking more than one subjects right away (I'm speakme savory casseroles and delectable desserts). Haha

Are you oven baking chicken thighs? Chop up some easy greens and roast them too. Baking bread for Sunday dinner? Throw collectively a cookie batter for dessert.

If you're paying to warmth the oven up, use it for all its properly properly well worth! It's basically the "run the machine whilst it's far entire" concept, but for baking. The trick is to pair ingredients or baked items that have comparable warm temperature requirements. Don't fear if the bread takes longer than the cookies. Just set one among a kind timers and pay interest.

Yeah, it does lessen the singular easy bread heady scent if you're which include on a sweet, too. But that is an good enough sacrifice to have extremely good baked items come out of the oven.

That wraps up the general cash saving utility hacks. Now it's time to get specific. Seasonally specific.

Summer

I live in the Mildly Southern United States but it may get fairly heat. Here are a few pointers we've got got picked as tons as maintain it cool in the summer time.

Turn up the thermostat!

This is without problems the maximum green way of saving coins inside the summer season, but allow's be sincere. Living sweaty is uncomfortable. That is why we have accrued several hints that will help you make the maximum of moderating your power use through AC.

Put the blankets away!!!

There is a time for weighted blankets, and August ain't it, woman! Put that in some huge tupperware and throw it inside the closet. Summer time is for the sheets.

My husband and I observed out early on now not to share blankets. We every have a iciness time blanket and a summer season sheet. If you have to understand, we have been recounted to rock the dinosaur blankies and Harry Potter cowl (Goodwill famous, of direction). But you gained't capture both parents useless inside the ones come mid-summer season. We have our non-public separate sheets at that trouble. We ain't hoping for no Midsummer Night fever goals.

Most commonplace birthday in the US? September nine. Why? I ain't no sociologist, however I wager it's far because of the reality it's so plenty more comfortable to be snuggly at the side of your hubby inside the middle of wintry climate. Save the cuddling for the pool because of the truth summer season loving genuinely aint it all of the time. Especially no longer in bed. Get your sheets and enjoy your area.

Now, don't get me wrong: sexual intimacy is surprisingly important for healthy marriages. Just find locations to cuddle without the AC blaring to make it arise any time. Try cold showers, doggystyle inside the the the front of the AC, or embody ice play surely to hold the attractive going regardless of what temperature it's far.

Now this may without a doubt be one of these moments in which you located "This lady achieved out of place her mind. I ain't THAT cheap." That's cool. There's a restrict to that complete "Would you do x for y amount of cash?" And for us, X = sweat it out a touch and Y = a couple of bucks on the AC invoice.

But if you are splurging in summer time and in spite of the reality that snuggling under quilts, your consolation level be too much!

One problem you could strive even as saving on AC but in spite of the truth that preserving the attractive: Schedule date nights. Yeah, setting sex on the calendar isn't usually sexy. But whats up, if you don't make it a topic, it is able to without issues fall off the normal. And that could be a courting ruiner. The sexiest sex is the intercourse that takes place (in region of the intercourse we want we had been having). So time table a date night.

Why? Because then you could splurge a touch on the AC with the aid of turning it down. Dim the lighting, flip the air up virtually a bit, and get comfortable. Then bypass once more in your coins saving conduct whilst the cuddle-sesh is finished.

Chapter 4: Buy a kiddie pool

Yeah, you apprehend the plastic tubs I'm speaking about. They may also moreover look goofy but it isn't simplest for the children. Last summer time I'd watch the children play on the same time as I gardened, however as soon as I had been given too pregnant, I stopped weeding and started out out soaking with them.

This is in which my favored comic, Mitch Hedberg, had been given it wrong.

"I noticed a business for an above-floor pool, it was 30 seconds prolonged. Because it virtually is the most amount of time you can image yourself having a laugh in an above-ground pool. If it have become 31 seconds, the actor might say "The water is only as a lot as right proper here? What do I do now? Throw the ball decrease again to Jimmy? Or placed a few goggles on and take a look at his toes?""

Let me let you realise. You don't ought to have a whole in-floor swimming pool with the intention to cool off within the summer time.

If you don't have dogs or chickens that have poppable claws, get a blow-up pool (however additionally get chickens - lifestyles is better with chickens). Otherwise, pick out up a plastic one from the shop and experience (skip in advance and get the chickens and tough plastic)!

You don't ought to refill it each and on every occasion due to the fact that might get steeply-priced. Just make sure to keep it rather easy through scooping out fall-ins and wiping off ft earlier than getting into. I'll admit, having the youngsters run inside and outside after freshly mowing the grass is considerably traumatic.

Money-saving-bonus-tip: If you're regularly refilling to keep away from constantly deciding on out floaties, take a few greater mins to bucket it in your garden plant life. Check out how gardening can keep your family even extra within the first ebook of this series. Snag it on Amazon right here.

But critically, although it is genuinely criss bypass applesauce inside the kiddie pool with a little one on your lap, do it! It is so exciting and permits beat the heat. If the water gets too warmth, feeling closer to bathwater shared with the aid of way of the whole circle of relatives, try setting it underneath a tree or refilling simply as needed to keep the water cooler.

Husband: I'm now not a huge fan of kiddie swimming pools, but I've been in it some instances. One of my personal desired hold cool in summer time topics does involve water. I'll genuinely hop in the shower and turn the water at the coldest placing for some seconds. It's a pleasant fresh wonder in your device and helped maintain me cool even if we had the thermostat set to eighty or 80 (yeah, that's what it have become like within the summer time in our condo).

Line dry clothes

Told you we'd talk about this.

When I became a infant, I endure in mind my mother hanging out smooth bed sheets. Core reminiscence! They seemed so magical blowing lightly within the wind (but the fact I in all likelihood peed on them the night earlier than). I'd peek and hide inside the gently swaying Lion King dual sheets, walking round due to the fact the wind vertically tucked me in time and again. There is truely a few issue specific approximately line drying garments within the outside. Not to say the cash it saves.

This saves coins in three strategies. The first is with the useful resource of the utilization of actually no longer walking the dryer. Have you ever noticed your lighting fixtures dim for 1/2 of a 2nd after starting a load? It's because of the truth the dryer is an energy guzzling gizmo that humans had been given by manner of way of tremendous without for the records of garments carrying up until 1937. You can maintain this money in some unspecified time inside the future of the summer season with the useful resource of setting garments outdoor.

The second manner it saves cash at some point of the summer season is thru not heating the residence. Think approximately it. You spend coins to warmth the dryer, but then that warm temperature dissipates slowly into your home, therefore changing the temperature internal - albeit ever so slightly. If it's far in particular heat and you're walking the AC, you are spending cash on cooling to counteract the warmth of the dryer. Silly!

The zero.33 way putting garments saves coins is with the useful resource of getting you and your circle of relatives outside. Humans had been made to be out of doors (except in intense climate) and we constantly think that outdoor time is outstanding spent at a park or some thing. Just circulate out of doors with the kids and hold at the gas money you'd spend with the aid of the use of traveling to the park. It might not appear to be a exquisite deal, however we've got had instances wherein gasoline prices have skyrocketed, making even a clean journey to the park a penny-pinching experience.

Just kidding. There are 4 strategies that setting clothes outside to dry saves you cash. It allows you to spend a whole lot lots much less cash on garments regular with 12 months. The dryer is an incredibly immoderate region. All that warmness and jostling?

The dryer consequently takes a large toll on garments. By putting off that greater friction and warmth, you can growth the sturdiness of your preferred blouse. Be positive to comply with me as an creator on Amazon so that you can get the alternative clothes saving secrets and techniques and strategies and strategies in Frugal Living for Parents: How to Save Money on Clothes, Entertainment, and Self-Care.

Take a note from moms of the despair generation and draw close them up!

Bonus tip: the sun can really dispose of stains without a doubt. Save a couple of bucks on stain remover.

Cook outside

Who doesn't love a terrific cookout? Summertime is for BBQ. Why? Because it's far too warm to prepare dinner inner. Plus, you could seat a ton of human beings on the garden. These are the exact methods you could save cash on utilities.

When you operate the oven inside the residence, you're essentially heating up the residence (equal concept as the dryer), however you get food at the element. Any warm temperature energy you positioned right right right into a tool modifications the equilibrium of the device. If that is an oven on your kitchen, your kitchen may be heated too to attain equilibrium. If your kitchen is heated, your own home will too. So what does your temperature tool do? Kicks on the AC a hint tougher. We may not physically notice it an excessive amount of, but our electric powered powered invoice does.

Save the baking for wintry climate. Cook out of doors within the direction of the summer season.

But the flies! I sense ya. So traumatic! If you are serving food out of doors, choose out up some food covering nets. Then set out a peace plate.

What is a peace plate? It's food you provide to the flies as a sacrifice. If they are busy eating otherwise undisturbed meals, there is probably a whole lot less flies interested in the meals in your plate. Yeah, you cannot have invited them, but serve them except to keep the peace. Not making fantastic some received't attempt on human plates and get stuck in the ghetto potato salad from the prepared-deli segment. Yeah, I'm a premade potato salad hater, however I consume it besides.

The 2nd way BBQing outdoor saves cash isn't continually on utilities. You are capable of get collectively with own family and pals and devour in a snug placing. Kids play. Grown-united statesvisit. This removes the need for accruing a big restaurant bill. Think about how an awful lot cash is stored with the aid of BBQing a slab of meat in desire to ordering person plates from a eating place for all your friends and circle of relatives.

That's obvious, but I don't have a huge backyard inclusive of you're speaking about. That's outstanding. Go to a park! So many have those little grills you may borrow if you name the town and reserve or surely flow into via first come, first serve. But I don't even recognize a way to paintings one of these. To be honest, me neither. YouTube to the rescue!

Chapter 5: Buy an Instant Pot

Along the identical strains as cooking out of doors, you need to discover strategies you may put together dinner without overly heating your own home. This is in which the Instant Pot comes in.

We had been given ours even as living in our tiny rental so honestly my first concept have turn out to be ungratefully, "Where the heck is that this detail going to move?"

Since then, I in reality have come to recognise its usefulness. I am now not this form of instantpot-or-die form of humans at the side of you meet within the Facebook agencies, however it does have its charge. It has changed our crock pot, rice cooker, and pressure cooker (whats up look, it did maintain area). But the fine characteristic is that it doesn't warmth the kitchen as a terrific deal.

Yes, in case you are using the stress function and you release it, it blows heat, humid air into the room, but it takes hundreds a lot a whole lot less power to warmth up than an oven or stovetop does.

Set it under the variety earlier than cooking. Once it is time to launch the pressure, spark off the fan and allow it cope with the brand new steam.

Plant some wood!

I'm pretty positive if I bit the bullet and paid for this kind of ancestry kits, it'd reveal I'm 1% Native American, 30% white and sixty nine% hippie. Not a complete-blown hippie however sufficient to encompass tree planting as a manner to maintain coins.

How? Granted, it isn't an right now cash saver, but over time it'll be bringing in the financial economic financial savings. Again, how? Because you'll have it made in the colour!

By planting deciduous timber (the timber that lose their leaves, really fertilizing your lawn and presenting homes for overwintering caterpillars - aka hen meals), you create a summer season cowl that cools your property.

So you're pronouncing I ought to surely plant a tree within the front backyard? Yes! If your out of doors is at the south or west element of your property. See, tree placement subjects. By planting on the south, west, or southwest aspect, you're developing an mind-set with the solar that casts a shadow on your home. Shady home = cooler domestic. Bonus factors for shaded concrete. Concrete acts as a warmth sponge so setting a cowl of leaves above it blocks it from the blazing warmth of direct daytime, for that reason reducing the temperature of your home average.

But you need to pick out trees that lose their leaves. Once the cooler weather devices in, the fallen leaves make way for the solar to polish via, consequently heating your home as hundreds as feasible within the wintry weather climate.

Get rid of the dang lawn!

I am very masses anti-lawn, and in reality, I experience it's miles interested by precise motive. Ok, possibly now not all lawn. It does look exquisite as a body for lawn beds. Plus it's miles first-rate to position out for a few yoga. But there may be in reality too much turf grass in suburban America and it can be costing you coins you surely don't must spend. Welcome to my list of four reasons why your lawn sucks (I recommend, I am awesome yours seems lovely - mass lawns in fashionable virtually suck).

1) You can't consume it

Lawns are a manufactured from 1700's Europe Flex. They had been born at a time at the equal time as wealthy humans ought to manipulate to pay for to plant their land with grasses that servants or livestock tended - as dang ornament! It changed into the signal of wealth. You need to give you the cash for to increase unnecessary grass in location of plant life for survival. How lush! And however we although perpetuate this whole "retaining up with the Joneses" agency. Silly!

Nowadays, our lawns are a sign of fulfillment. The American Dream comes with the residence surrounded by manner of what? A pristine inexperienced lawn that says your weekend hours. Or you pay servants to govern.

This equal garden can be used as region to increase food for you.

But I'm now not a gardener. Besides, isn't it some of work?

I concentrate ya. Most human beings think of gardening as rototilling the soil and massive patches of dirt you've got got to devise and set up each 365 days. This doesn't need to be so! By planting fruit wood and berry timber, you located in the paintings once (planting) and get fed for years. You might also truly want to wait some to get fruit. But I promise: the wait is nicely well worth it.

But we probable obtained't even live in this equal house in some years. Plant it besides! We commonly like to speak approximately how we need to be kind to others. Random acts of kindness, proper? Holding open the door. Texting that pal. Sending your mate plants as it's Wednesday.

But what about acts of kindness that pass past time? Planting a tree now that allows you to feed someone else later? That's the form of affection this international goals. Yeah, a grin perks a person's day, but a tree planted now's a blessing for years to come! This can be my hippie statistics displaying, however plant a tree now and your kindness lives an awful lot longer than a grin or open door.

2)   It is America's largest irrigated crop, and for what? You can't devour it!

It is actually America's largest irrigated crop. If extraterrestrial beings came to visit and noticed what we have been doing with our land regions, they could chuckle, concluding there is no smart life on this planet. Unless you have pastures feeding livestock, your lawn sustains no existence and but we WATER IT LIKE CRAZY! It's insane!

I propose, I'm not anti-sprinkler, however fine if there are kids gambling in it. (Bonus tip - go to your local splash park in vicinity of the usage of your very personal sprinkler. Let the metropolis pay for the water whilst you and unique families experience the shared place!)

three)   It prices your time and money to keep it manicured and mowed.

Remember those weekend hours we mentioned? That is taking some time away. Honestly, if you can make more money performing some component else in the quantity of time it takes to mow a garden, pay a person else to mow the lawn due to the fact you will no matter the truth that be receiving a internet profits.

four)   It gives no longer some thing for the man or woman round you

When humans need to keep nature, you receive as proper with you studied of them as those who have polar undergo screensavers or filled pandas as their "maintain-the-world" mascot. However, our biodiversity is declining a excellent deal toward domestic. Urban sprawl has considerably faded the herbal regions in which plants that maintain vegetation and fauna thrive. Take a test Google Earth. Flip via the notable timelines on the regions close to you. We are abruptly increasing our reaches with pavement, houses, and you guessed it: lawn. And for what? To preserve up with stated Joneses like 1700 slave-proprietors? Come on, we're higher than that.

So what are we presupposed to do if we don't have a garden? Onto the subsequent coins saving point!

Chapter 6: Plant local flowers instead

Did you understand it takes a own family of chickadees 6,000-9,000 caterpillars to decorate a capture of birds? And in which do they get the ones caterpillars? Certainly not the garden!!! Most bugs are professionals, that means they advanced to quality devour one or certain varieties of plants that advanced alongside them. If those vegetation aren't in our region, we won't have the birds that consume the ones professional caterpillars each.

That's all excellent, but it's miles a touch weird how passionate you are about this. How precisely will planting nearby flowers preserve me coins?

I understand. It is a hint bizarre. But allow me display you the 3 techniques it saves you money!

1)   It presents amusement proper out of doors your the front door. I mean, we pay

coins to visit butterfly gardens. We've all seen the butterfly lawn brochures within the rotating tour brochure stand at Wendy's. You can grow one outdoor. Right out your window! We pay cash in gasoline to strain to trekking spots to connect with nature. We can hook up with nature on the the the the the front porch.

Do your kids want pets? Do they have already got pets and but ask for more? Plant a few o.K.Trees or milkweed. Attract their modern pets. Because while you begin planting their food belongings, they'll come. If you preserve up their meals assets, they will live. As Doug Tallemy, one of my hippie heroes with the credentials to again it up, writes in his ebook Natures' Best Hope, that cardinal you spot out of doors feeding at the caterpillars you planted natives for is your cardinal. You don't even want to cage it or easy its poop tray. It lives round you because you take care of it. Easiest pets regarded to guy!

2)   The 2d manner planting natives saves you coins is observed for your water invoice. Native flora are flora that were born for your area. It advanced to grow in handiest this kind of water scenario. Desert plants can live at the wilderness with out you slaving over it with a hose. After the primary year of tending to it in its "infancy," you in reality in no way want to water it yet again. They had been made to live in the elements. Your particular region's factors.

three)   Another way community vegetation shop cash - they last. Native plant life are designed to stay for your particular area so that you obtained't should infant them. Unlike one of a kind vegetation which could get worn out except overly blanketed from weather or pests, natives will thrive to your out of doors. And if you buy perennials (the flora that cross decrease lower back year after 12 months), you could hold your lawn beds all in favour of out buying vegetation again and again each spring.

four)   No insecticides or fertilizers - You don't should create a false environment for community vegetation and that they obtained't succumb to pests they might't address. So I obtained't have any insects on my neighborhood plants? Not real! They can be smorgasmorging to your community plants. But that dinner party is the dinner party that allows your local flowers and fauna. Take your chook trying to the subsequent diploma with the aid of using installing nature's hen feeders proper outdoor your door.

But I hate bugs!

I concentrate you. But do you absolutely? Let's consider it for a 2d. Do you hate frogs? Do you hate butterflies? All of these items need insects to thrive. We aren't speakme approximately planting natives for roaches or maggots. Those are after your pantries - now not your gardens. When we plant natives, we're enhancing our network biodiversity with beneficial pollinators. Ain't no person too mad about growing populations of lightning bugs and butterflies.

But shouldn't we keep away from encouraging nature in our neighborhoods? Like, isn't that for native parks and stuff?

Why? Especially when you have a backyard that dreams plants otherwise it becomes a dirt bowl. To examine greater, I virtually advise reading Nature's Best Hope via Doug Tallemy. It is so correct!

five)	Last reason why neighborhood plant life save you cash:

Your location may additionally moreover pay you to plant natives for pollinators. Minnesota has launched a software program paying you the price to turn your lawn into wildflowers and natives to prevent specialized bee extinction. There are presently insects across the country dwindling in numbers, however Minnesota modified into the number one to take initiative. Let's skip Minnesota! And allow's hold pushing for special states to look at healthy, we could?

I in reality recognize the HOA factor of view and keeping housing charges as excessive as possible, but there can be a thing wherein we understand that human beings aren't the first-class species to fear about. If bugs skip, via an complicated but quick moving way, we pass too. What would not it absorb your community to start understanding that and installing their non-public utility to pay owners?

#ThankYouForComingToMyTedTalk

Alright, I can see how these sort of utility cash-saving-hints might in all likelihood assist supply prices down, but what if I don't need to be sweating day in and day ride. I propose, I need to be snug.

I pay attention ya. These techniques are truely now not diva evidence (no longer, which you are or some component - but if you are, I ain't judging). Onto the following cash-saving existence hack.

Go sun

The previous strategies had been all delicate through my husband and I looking for to reduce prices in our appreciated condominium. We sweated, ate popsicles, and left the house windows open as regularly as we have to genuinely to keep our payments underneath $a hundred. But now, we've had been given solar.

Now, sun actually isn't unfastened. We ought to pay monthly for the loan on our setup. And it's not particularly reasonably-priced both.

However, it in fact isn't the worst. And we can rely on regular electric powered powered bills - no surprises.

Some locations can pay you for the strength you generate and don't use. We sadly don't stay in such an area, but the transition was even though nicely properly really worth it.?

But in case you live in a place that doesn't pay you to your generated strength, why problem?

Why trouble?! This can be the primary summer time we will truely splurge and use a comforter inside the center of August. We can cuddle on the sofa inside the path of film night time time. We can maintain out the area sleeve shirts if we need. And we will need to worry about no longer some thing finance-clever!

I can't inform you how excited I am. Yeah, is sun cheap? No, however the rate we pay is constant regardless of how a good deal we use it and we aren't paying extra than we'd otherwise.

Solar programs variety through area and electric powered powered powered business organisation, so really test out how topics paintings in your region. If you're lucky sufficient to stay in an area if you want to pay you on your extra energy, you can though be remarkable frugal together together with your power usage after which be paid on your unused electricity. Talk approximately prevailing!

You don't produce as masses in wintry climate despite the fact that, so that is a few element to keep in thoughts. It is solar based totally definitely and counting on in which you stay, the sun simply isn't as available 12 months-round.

Husband: I do have some subjects to say about solar.

1. Our monthly payments are simply over ninety greenbacks a month on a 20-year loan. The desirable information is that our hobby rate is a whopping 0.Nine%. Yeah, a lot less than 1%. Less than the traditional inflation charge. We do although pay a flat fee to our electricity employer for being linked to the grid (12 dollars a month).

2. We do get "sun credit" for extra power going decrease back into the grid, so at the same time as there isn't an instantaneous financial gain, this does complement us at some stage in the months of tons less Sun.

3. If you're thinking about solar, don't virtually go along with the primary ad you phrase on Facebook or Google. Shop round a piece and get some costs. We

stored over 9000 greenbacks with the useful resource of purchasing round (evaluating the very best quote to the lowest).

4. There are although a few authorities tax incentives for going solar. We were given some thousand decrease again on our tax move back closing yr and a few this 12 months too. The amount you can get decrease returned goes down each yr, so time is of the essence.

So what can I do at some point of the iciness months? Let's talk approximately it.

Winter

We've already blanketed a way to live on most important warmness waves with cash although to your pocket, but what about wintry weather?

Onward!

Bundle up

If you live in a less warm vicinity, there are a few options for staying heat. Gas heating, wooden heating, a few element else heating, or being a undergo. I preference with each fiber of my being that we want to hibernate the wintry climate away, but as it's miles, we lamentably can not. Instead, we should pay to warm temperature our houses. Naturally, the amazing way to keep money is to maintain the dial on a cooler than everyday temperature.

But that is right enough. Why? Because you can with out trouble bundle deal up. My preferred excuse I pay interest human beings say at the same time as talking about how winter is their favored season is "In wintry climate, you could positioned on layers to live heat. In summer season, you could be naked and it's miles though warmth." Fair sufficient. Good argument -

despite the fact that the incorrect thing. Summer is first-rate. Fight me! :P

Wearing layers is the perfect way to maintain coins. Buy some second hand sweaters, thermals, and a modern day package deal deal of socks (I genuinely can't do the complete 2nd hand socks issue - extra on how to shop coins on garments within the next e book).

Girl, I higher in no manner trap you turning the dial up in only a t-blouse. If you're wearing a blouse, sweater, thermal pants, an overlay of pajama pants, multiple snug socks, and you're however cold? Spend some time beneath a blanket with your loved one in advance than you attempt the thermostat all once more.

Ok, that sounds sort of excessive. How bloodless is in reality too cold?

The World Health Organization recommends an indoor temperature of as a minimum sixty 4-tiers Fahrenheit. If you have babies, elderly, or immunocompromised people living in your private home, then it's far encouraged to keep it at 70 stages.

Anything decrease and it's far too bloodless for our our our our bodies. But a few issue higher and you are paying greater for consolation. Just layer up!

If you're out of the house for an extended term, you ought to show your heating unit off, proper? Wrong! That have to reason pipes to leak and home gadget to interrupt, resulting in a big restore bill. Before you leave, flip the dial to a balmy 50 tiers Fahrenheit and phone it accurate for the adventure.

Chapter 7: Rice packs

Want to recognize the maximum ghetto but inexperienced trick to warming your fingers interior? Taking a as an opportunity more today's sock (forget about about the stinky, grimy ones - they may most effective get stinkier and dirtier on this repurposement), filling it up with rice, tying off the pinnacle, and throwing it inside the microwave for a minute or two.

Out comes a lovable ball of warmth that lasts quite a while. You may want to use this trick on the identical time as cuddled beneath a blanket, looking tv. This works fantastic in bed!

When we lived in our 6 year rental, it became draft-ridden and cold one December - the December I had to finish my time period paper at the information of calculus, to be unique. I will in no manner understand how an collection of lifestyles picks landed me in the the the front of a laptop typing out the history of calculus. I had each excuse at my fingers to make me revel in depressing.

Want to recognize what helped maintain me typing in choice to flunking the class? My available-dandy rice ball. I microwaved a couple of those home made heaters. One to relaxation my feet on and the opportunity for my lap. Even although it come to be iciness (my least favored season), and I even have come to be succumbing to a calculus assignment (my least favored task), I placed a manner to hold it snug and incredible. All for masses a good deal much less than a couple of dollars!

These moreover paintings nicely for frame aches and pains. Heavy duration with hundreds of cramping? Rice sock! Lower back ache? Rice sock! Going on a hike inside the bloodless? Rice sock for your hoodie pocket!

So reasonably-priced and so snug!

Just ensure not to burn your self. They can get heat whilst right now on the skin. Because of this, don't be seeking to hold coins inside the crib with a rice sock. It may be volatile whilst too warmth with children. Always display any warmness source spherical your children. Protect your infants!

Insulate home home windows

Remember our loved 6 12 months condominium? It had wonderful Southern lights from a huge pull-thru glass door. But boy, end up that element bloodless in the useless of winter! In truth, all the house windows had been first rate drafty within the vain of wintry weather.

They were probably particular home windows and the crack from an airborne Thomas the Train toy didn't assist any. We needed to discover a way to maintain those rented home home windows hotter.

Of direction, we study all approximately blankets. We covered the house home windows with blankets within the bed room and that did assist, however I didn't want to sacrifice that Southern sunshine! Dark and cold is an lousy lot worse than wonderful and bloodless.

Even if the temperature is in the negatives outdoor, strength from the sun warms your home through radiation. That adorable daylight hours, Baby! Put a blanket inside the the front of it and you lose that warm temperature/strength.

I had to provide you with each different plan.

Nothing an lousy lot takes area if you paste a blanket proper up against the window. Yeah, it'll assist a bit bit, but typically you'll virtually have a wet blanket due to the condensation. Now, when you have directly up, open drafts, certain blockading it will block the wind. It may even block the heated air from escaping thru the cracks.

However, as speedy as your drafts are looked after, it obtained't assist an entire lot to line the window with blankets. See, it's miles simply air that creates appropriate insulation. From your draft-loose window, keep near a blanket or set of heavy curtains a small distance away. That air trapped in a number of the window and the blanket creates a barrier of insulating air that without a doubt works.

But once more, the blanket blocks the lovable sun.

So we had to get progressive. Curtains art work well because of the reality you could pull them open at some degree within the day and near them at night time, letting the solar's magic come through. But if it's miles cold at some stage in the day, you're sacrificing that small barrier of insulation you'd get from keeping it up.

Why no longer each? Why no longer each! Here is the trick: bubble wrap. Bubble wrap is see via and presents that air area of insulation. Just tape a few up in your brightest home windows and you've got got got a translucent seal that we can also need to the slight in on the equal time as moreover insulating your private home.

Yeah, it is able to look a chunk ghetto but it's miles only for the cold season and it continues yall tremendous and snug without unnecessary power spikes.

Bubble wrap can be luxurious, however you may start gathering from shipping programs.

Or improve your home's windows if it's miles in your price range. It's probable lots more efficient besides, but if this ain't the season for that, bubble wrap!

Chapter 8: Switch the direction of the ceiling fan

Most human beings apprehend approximately this one, but my husband and I clearly however warfare every yr. It's like voodoo magic or some detail (I clearly have a physics degree and even though war with the concept)! We want to google each season which manner your ceiling fan should waft. I'm pretty excellent we caught ourselves more than one times using our ceiling fan the wrong manner for the incorrect season. Like, the complete time!

Don't be like us. Learn to comprehend that little activate the issue and feature your fan developing the precise air go with the go along with the waft for an appropriate season.

Just don't request from me how. I'm no longer 100% positive ours are presently set efficaciously.

Husband: Looking up from beneath the fan: Clockwise in the wintry weather. Counter-clockwise within the summer time. You shouldn't experience any fan air coming down at once on you in the wintry weather, you need the air to go along with the flow upwards. Yes, I in reality googled it and sure, 1 out of the 5 fanatics in our residence have been going the incorrect way.

Baths!

Ok, baths aren't necessarily reasonably-priced to have finally of the iciness. After all, you're spending coins on every water and gas to warmth it. But there may be not anything more relaxed than an extended soak within the middle of frostbite-prepared out of doors temperatures.

But proper right here is the money saving hack. Don't pull the plug. Once you get out of the tub, depart the water there until it runs bloodless. When you right now drain it after toweling off, you permit your hard earned coins flush down the drain, warming the pipes within the floor in choice to your home.

Think approximately it: you already paid to warmth that water. That water holds warm temperature energy. By looking ahead to the water to head bloodless earlier than draining, that warmth energy warms your rest room and slowly your house. Similar to the dryer scenario we mentioned in advance. As an introduced bonus, the moisture provides humidity to your home, that is extensively wanted for the duration of seasons while heating gadgets run, depleting the moisture in your private home.

Trust me on this: acquire your hand within the icy water later to enjoy savoring the warmth you already spent cash on.

Now, if you have greater younger children or others who want to results fall and drown in the water, DO NOT USE THIS TRICK! Saving a few cents is in no way properly well worth the danger of loss of life. But when you have older children in which the simplest danger is that they use it for an indoor wintry weather nerf outstanding soaker warfare, this is first-class.

Husband: Don't be afraid to percentage bathwater as properly. If you are definitely soaking its no longer going to get that dirty. I continuously use my spouse's bathwater (its though clearly heat for me even as she receives out). Just don't go in after she shaves her legs.

Get lively

Know why you shiver whilst you're cold? Because your frame is privy to that shifting produces warm temperature, elevating your body temperature. You can harness this strength your self! Move spherical. Get your blood flowing. This will assist stay warm on days you'd need to crank the heater all over again as lots as 78 or some thing your move-to temperature is.

I recognize it is a whole lot greater cushty to sit down underneath a weighted blanket along side your rice sock for your lap, ingesting cereal or some aspect. But there can be a time for that and once more for getting active.

That doesn't even necessarily recommend getting out the p90x films. Have a closet that desires decluttering? Don't wait till spring (that's gardening season)! Do it now! Decluttering, cleaning, rearranging furniture. All of it facilitates you feel warmer in some unspecified time in the future of cold seasons.

You have the ones big dreams within the over again of your mind that you want to get finished. Get them finished in the path of the wintry climate months! Reward yourself with a task nicely completed by means of manner of the use of snuggling underneath the blanket with a rice sock AFTER you've long lengthy beyond thru and prepared the tupperware that tumbles out the cupboard each time you attain for a few element down there.

Chapter 9: Throw rugs

I love tough wooden flooring. They are the best backdrop for throw rugs. Throw rugs now not satisfactory make rooms study ease, but within the route of the wintry weather, they assist rooms enjoy at ease. Whether you live on a slab or a crawlspace, placing a rug down to your tough flooring will drastically heat up the location.

We have been able to find out all our rugs off Facebook marketplace or storage income for drastically reasonably-priced. We clearly have more than one shag rugs within the garage for at the same time as the children play in there. Don't underestimate the power of the shag!

Cook interior

You apprehend Jesus wasn't born in December, proper? Know why we've got an amazing time his birthday then?

Because it is too dang warm to be oven roasting a ham in the summer season! Haha, truely kidding. It probably had to do with the reality that it have become an awful lot less tough to convert pagans to Christianity inside the event that they blended their antique traditions with celebrations of Jesus.

But critically, iciness is the time for proper baking! Homemade breads, cookies, casseroles, roasted meat, all of it! It is so comforting to examine the dreary weather from interior an oven heated domestic, wafting with sweet smells of pastries.

If you don't have toddlers taking walks round, you could open the oven door at the same time as the meals comes out and permit it heat the air spherical you. If you want to shut it, that's actual enough too. It will although warmness the residence, sincerely at a slower, much less vital price.

Never tried to put together dinner your non-public inventory in advance than? Let a pot simmer on the stovetop for more than one hours. The warm temperature and moisture creates a snug temperature within the kitchen with the bonus of savory smells at some point of the house.

Not fine will soups heat the kitchen with delicious steam, but it warms your frame too. Eating warm soups, consuming hot tea, taking warm baths. It all warms the frame in addition to the soul.

Plant evergreen wood

More bushes? Seriously?

More bushes! But a splendid type and in a remarkable place this time. Evergreen bushes are the kind that don't lose their leaves each fall. These timber act as super windbreakers at the same time as planted on the north thing of your house (the place of your planting topics here too).

This wind ruin blocks iciness chills from tumbling over your house. It considerably cuts fee down on heating while there can be a wall of evergreens popularity defend to the north.

Transportation

If you're some component like me, you live in an American place with room for improvement on public transportation. For maximum of my vicinity, a car is the workhorse for the working man. So right right here we are going to start out with our cash saving tips for cars. And to be sincere, I excellent had been given suggestions for saving cash on vehicles.

Buy used

You apprehend what sounds superb? Getting a BRAND NEW CAR [insert Bob Barker voice-over for full effect]. Know what isn't first-rate? The masses of greenbacks it depreciates at the same time as riding it out of the automobile dealership [insert depressing splash of reality and seemingly endless payments for full effect].

I understand why humans want cutting-edge vehicles. Who doesn't want the relaxation of no car problems for a twelve months or even as underneath guarantee? And all the electric powered powered abilities that would skip incorrect make any little vehicle restore some thing best a representative can control.

However, you better do your research inside and outside earlier than getting a vehicle new. A cousin of ours offered a emblem-new truck after timing the marketplace and profits and one of a kind witchcraft to make it a good buy.

Unless you're an vehicle wizard like that with the manner to spit out the half of-a-residence fee on a automobile, buy used.

But how can I ensure I don't get a hunk-a-junk? You can't. But the following tip lets in.

Chapter 10: Research dependable producers

Look on the road. What motors appearance the dingiest and in want of a paint technique? If they're older than your kids and probably your diploma, this means that it's far a reliable automobile. We have usually supplied Hondas the beyond few instances due to the truth they were the most dependable manufacturers we've were given used.

Tried the Chryslers. Tried the Dodges. Tried the Lincolns (they do be snug despite the fact that). Nothing got here with the carefree reliability like a Honda (may additionally need to delete this - I enjoy like I actually gave away the solutions to those credit rating test quizzes).

Google "dependable family used vehicles." Get extra unique when you have top notch dreams. Start at the blogs for thoughts, then studies those cars and find out what others have to mention on forums. Spending the time now studying cars or vehicles with little extended-term issues will prevent cash in the end via way of a) searching for used and b) saving on steady automobile protection (in particular electric powered powered stuff).

Take care of your infant

The car is a member of your own family. It receives you from vicinity to vicinity and protects you inside the case of an on road collision. It's like a chauffeur/navy tank. Because it does loads on your nicely-being, it desires to be sorted.

Regularly service your car. Replace the tires. Change the oil. Wash it at the same time as it's far excessively dirty (I notwithstanding the truth that want to discover ways to do this one). This ordinary preservation will hold your vehicle on foot easily and increase its toughness. Who wouldn't want to inherit the automobile they used to have a booster seat inside the again? Maybe now not your youngster, but so what?! No one's first vehicle need to have a current day automobile heady scent without a swaying tree above the dashboard.

Name your vehicle

This can also additionally sound goofy however listen me out: we name topics we like. We name subjects we take care of. If you struggle to get your vehicle's oil modified constantly, provide her a name.

It's much less complicated neglecting a "Honda Civic" than it's miles a "Barbara." It's much less complicated to throw trash on a "Ford Focus" than it's far a "Frederick." It'd be much less difficult to smooth a "Brittany" than a "Toyota Camry."

If you battle with the renovation responsibilities required to preserve your vehicle in suitable form, try giving your vehicle a name. It should probably truely be the trick that keeps you responsible because it feels too awful to forget about approximately an "Orville" or whoever you have got were given were given parked out of doors.

Drive the rate limit

We are all responsible of speeding on occasion but let me will let you recognize motives that charge you. The first is a given: tickets are steeply-priced. My stepdad always gave this recommendation, "Drive as fast as you can have enough money." Not most effective are tickets now not cheap, however your insurance goes up after web website site visitors violations.

Bonus tip: if you are a accountable riding pressure, display it via getting one of these video show devices from your insurance that would reduce your charge for proper driving force-ness. We did that, and in spite of the reality that I do no longer assume we succeeded, it is extraordinary in concept and can prevent coins if you're that sort of character.

The 2nd way the usage of the rate restriction saves you coins is through gasoline mileage. The quicker you pass, the extra money you spend on fuel to hold your car at that pace.

Husband: The US Department of power and special states that for each "five mph you pressure over 50 mph is like paying a in addition $zero.25 in line with gallon for gasoline". They really have a neat calculator to discover the penalty in your make and model of vehicle. Check it here!

Keep an empty trunk

You recognize that bag of clothes you've been this means that to donate? Donate it! You are spending extra money on fuel to keep those round every and every strain.

One of my preferred brief testimonies (and the best that stimulated me as a more youthful character to need to put in writing sci-fi (search for new fiction books on my author net net page within the next three hundred and sixty five days or) is referred to as The Cold Equations. I've associated the PDF because it's a high-quality study when you have the time. (Plus, we're nearing the give up of the e-book and I don't want to go away you literature-much less once you've written an Amazon product examine for this book)!

If you don't have time, I'll summarize a bit. There's a spaceship on the manner to send scientific materials to human beings in need, and the gas for the supply is calculated basically all of the way down to the ultimate drop. However, at the manner, a stowaway woman is decided. There isn't enough gas to take her and so the warfare rises.

We have to recall our vehicles in that equal warfare. You are paying in fuel to transport some thing is to your car. If you're sporting a field of dishes your mother gave you because of the reality you don't apprehend what to do with them, do some element quick due to the fact you're actually spending money hauling that indecision!

Do you've got had been given a thousand pairs of little one shoes in the lower back? Clean them out due to the reality however the fact that they aren't heavy, you're however paying moderate portions to take them everywhere with you. It affords up.

Keep handiest what you want. Your children, your handbag, a number one useful beneficial aid kit, and some thing is critical for that particular enjoy. Your car isn't always a closet, so save you paying to haul random crap you don't want.

Husband: She must were looking within the over again of my vehicle while writing the above. Side study: I moreover had 4 gallons of cleaning soap yet again there (you recognize those massive jugs you operate to top off the little hand dispenser ones). Well, one busted and leaked anywhere. My vehicle smells FABULOUS now (and the trunk is a sticky mess). Moral of the tale – do away with what you don't want and genuinely contend with stuff as you get it.

Chapter 11: Have fine the vehicles you want

Extra vehicles in the circle of relatives may be available, but there may be now not anything wrong with selling one and downsizing if need be. You keep cash on coverage, taxes, it all. And life isn't the give up of the world if you don't have a car for every body inside the family. See what is inner walking distance of wherein you stay. Is there a bus prevent? Are there stores you could walk to? Pedestrian existence moreover has hidden fitness benefits that save you lots on healthcare as you age.

Husband: Back in my bachelor days, I had an antique sports activities vehicle (2-seater). Unfortunately, I had to say goodbye to her because it didn't make feel to keep it with a family (I absolutely couldn't placed a car seat in there). Bittercandy moment, however we did hold lots on insurance.

Mind your gasoline (and spoil) pedal

Now, that is a contact much like the entire "strain most effective as speedy as you can manage to pay for" deal, however it is a touch precise. Every time you press on the gas pedal, you're spending coins. You may not be getting out your credit score rating score card each and every time you accelerate, but each time you do, you use up the fuel you pay for. Therefore, you need to purchase greater.

This isn't rocket technology or a few trouble, however virtually considering dollar symptoms every time you press the gasoline pedal changes your driving behavior to be more money aware.

Another Nana story:

Like I said in the previous ebook in this series, I spent lots of time with my Nana. We traveled often. Sometimes lengthy distances, but most of the time to and from school. Being the younger teen who knew everything, it drove me loopy while she drove so slow up to a forestall slight. Like, it felt like we had been crawling to a prevent moderate. I never understood why she didn't virtually stay at her normal speed and then forestall like a normal individual.

"Why do you stress so gradual??" I groaned, truly in want of an mind-set check my Nana didn't deserve.

"Because there's a forestall signal."

"But the stop sign is to this point away, and we are going so slow!"

"You should gradual all of the way down to prevent."

"Yeah, however no longer till you get there!!!" I truly don't recognize how I in no manner have been given popped within the mouth with the ones crinkled arthritis fingers.

It have become most effective later in existence I understood how clever she became. It charges cash to keep your foot at the fuel pedal, and in case you are searching the slight turn yellow up earlier at the same time as keeping the equal pace to get there, you're spending coins if it takes the fuel pedal to do it.

Chapter 12: What Is Being Frugal?

Money is comprised of paper but doesn't broaden on bushes. This can be as an alternative apparent, however it elements to the fact that money isn't easy to come back via. You need to art work difficult for it. This also can comprise prolonged hours within the administrative center, call center, or something manner you're busy doing. Once your paycheck arrives, you revel in a revel in of achievement from all the try which you installed to get it. However, the cash you acquired won't be with you for all time. You will should use it to pay your payments and precise expenses. You also can in the end spend this all up speedy. Then your subsequent paycheck comes and you rinse and repeat the cycle again and again.

While you could live with this way for the rest of your lifestyles, ultimately you begin to apprehend that there's a few element crucial which you ought to be doing. You need to be saving coins. The transmission goes on the auto, you get harm in a freak accident or honestly unwell and need time away from artwork. Saving cash is important for buying prepared for sudden emergencies. Having money can also be vital to the way you'll spend your retirement years. Knowing this, you comprehend that you need to discover techniques to preserve cash from draining out of your monetary organization account. While looking the net, you take place to come across the phrase "frugal."

Frugal may be defined as being careful with spending cash. This doesn't suggest being reasonably-priced or selfish. Being frugal is a sensible description for individuals who care about the price in their cash. Frugal human beings recognize that cash really can't visit waste. Hence, they find methods to maintain as a minimum a component of their income. Eventually, these little economic monetary savings turn out to be of remarkable help to them in future years.

Being frugal isn't clean. There may be many temptations and worrying situations so one can come your manner. After all, it's far a natural inclination whilst we have were given more money to spend it. Nevertheless, in making ready for the frugal way of life, you should equip yourself with some key tendencies and tendencies so that you will be a success.

Have a set mindset

You need to acquire and persuade yourself to participate in a frugal way of lifestyles. No one need to stress you into this manner of residing. You need to appearance the benefits of being frugal and encompass the techniques related to it. If you aren't happy of the concept, your tries to being frugal might also moreover simply fail and backfire. It all starts offevolved offevolved at the aspect of your mindset.

Know your desires

You want to understand why you need to be frugal. Do some research on what you may do at the side of your monetary financial financial savings and approaches your coins can increase. Simply being frugal isn't sufficient to inspire you to maintain being frugal. You ought to have plans on precisely what you need to do with the coins. Whether it's far for emergency finances or your retirement vacations, having a easy reason may want to significantly help for your frugal lifestyle. Of path, it might be higher if you shared those goals with whoever can be stricken by your frugality. Your associate and kids want to apprehend what exactly drives you to be frugal. In a way, you can try to persuade them to sign up for you closer to achieving those desires.

Determination

As stated in advance, there could be trials in order to check your frugality. You may additionally moreover see gadgets which you actually need to buy but you manifestly recognize might be simply useless or will derail your plans to achieve your intention. You may want to probable should refuse eating in risky fast food chains. Even worse, first-rate humans may also ridicule you and claim which you are too stringent.

Amidst all of the traumatic situations that you may face, you want to preserve happening with what you receive as true with in. You shouldn't surrender so you have a threat to obtain some issue desires you've got got in thoughts. After all, you keep in mind that the ones is probably of awesome advantage to you and your circle of relatives in the future.

Be Creative

Many frugal humans exercise unconventional techniques to hold cash. You will need to innovate and expect out of doors the sphere a good way to find out strategies to keep your cash and reduce costs. Fortunately, many books (like this one!) and others concerning frugal dwelling have already been published. Hence, with the right assets and your private efforts, you may exercising frugality.

Chapter 13: Being Frugal At Home

The home is one of the first regions we should appearance to on the identical time as thinking about making changes to live greater frugally. Creating a incredible home surroundings is critical. Knowing that your own home will obviously be an vital a part of your existence, you have to maximize the software program of this region. Here is wherein you rest and bond with family people. Outside of that, all strategies like eating, taking showers and particular necessities take location right right here. However, near your own home, many charges can come along. Taxes, bills, and different payments are required so you can maintain this sanctuary. You ought to search for ways to limit those crucial costs and ease the monetary burden that your area of residence brings.

Being frugal with your house doesn't suggest making it substandard. There are many possible techniques to cut expenses or maybe decorate the residence surroundings. This chapter will talk some of those thoughts that you may recall.

1.Try to search for a smaller residence or rental. Even if you could have sufficient cash a big house, you can however be frugal with the useful aid of selecting a smaller one instead. This may additionally want tons less protection and can additionally fee a good deal much less. As lengthy as your family can correctly live in it, you can certainly revel in this at ease domestic.

2.Plant wood. To reduce the warm temperature absorbed by manner of your private home, you could do not forget setting trees round your private home. This have to reduce your want for air con. Also, this may provide higher air flow for your property.

3.Turn off the lights and computer systems. Even those clean steps may assist in decreasing the rate of your strength invoice. When you need to move away the room, turn the lighting fixtures off. When you're completed with the laptops and computer structures shop your artwork and electricity them down.

four.Have a complete freezer. Empty freezers may additionally need extra power to hold a cold temperature. If you in reality don't have some thing to position inside the freezer, you could fill jugs with water and place those on your freezer. As greater vicinity is used, less power might be required to maintain the ones cool.

5.Unplug. If an gadget is plugged right into a wall socket, it'd although draw out a few shape of electricity. This can slowly increase your electric powered powered invoice. As a good buy as possible, unplug all appliances whilst you aren't the use of them. These little actions can also decide how plenty you'll store at the equal time as your electric powered bill arrives.

6.Clean the coils of your refrigerator. The coils in the lower back of your fridge can turn out to be dusty after a while. This need to cause your refrigerator to artwork tougher and consume more strength. This can also need to extend the life of your refrigerator and make it use a whole lot much less power.

7.Do it yourself maintenance. If a few factor in the house isn't working, you can attempt to learn how to recuperation the ones issues. Instead of hiring a repairman, you can keep greater through your non-public hard paintings. Such data may also be beneficial for destiny situations. There are such plenty of DIY blogs, you tube films and books in the present day age there can be probably a step by step manual to pretty masses any in the course of the house project. Here is a list of 17 of the higher DIY blogs to get you commenced out http://huff.To/1FXB9RT

8.Keep the blinds and curtains closed. This can help with the insulation of your property. Hence, it would be fine inside the course of cold weather. Of path, even as the weather is warm, do open these to permit air circulate in your property.

nine.Clean the clear out of air conditioners and furnaces. More green domestic gadget might need a good deal much less electricity. This can also then equate to decrease strength payments. It is probably wonderful to easy the ones in advance than the seasons on the identical time as they're wished. That way, they'll be straight away used at the identical time as essential.

10. Keep your property clean. This would possibly prevent coins as you will should

spend a good deal less on cleaning merchandise. In developing conduct to smooth your home each day, you could keep away from the assemble-up of dirt.

eleven. Make your very personal cleaning substances. If you find searching for cleansing merchandise high priced, you could additionally choose to create your personal cleansing substances. For example, common family materials like vinegar, baking soda, and dish cleansing soap all make effective own family cleaners for flooring.

12. Make brilliant that the air conditioners and furnaces are of the right period. If they may be too small, they might need to artwork more difficult. If they may be too large, they might truely lose performance and can use extra energy.

13. Use compact fluorescent bulbs. They may additionally to start with fee greater

than everyday bulbs, however they might display to be beneficial in the long run. They can last up to 10 instances longer than the ordinary mild bulb. Other than that, they could want much less power.

14. If you operate a cell telephone, put off your landline. In this factor in time, maximum human beings are on cellular telephones. With this, landlines can grow to be impractical.

15. Don't rent a modem. It's better to shop for one than virtually rent. You is probably capable of hold more in the end.

sixteen. Use Google Docs or different online place of job applications. Instead of having to spend greater on extra talents like Microsoft Office, you can take benefit of unfastened options available online.

17. Restore or construct fixtures. This would possibly make of a a laugh DIY mission. With the proper system and time,

you may maintain hundreds of coins. Moreover, you can be glad together with your private creations.

18. Use a clothes line. Instead of using a dryer, you can use the natural rays from the sun to dry your garments. This will preserve loads in energy and could help your garments final longer.

19. Let the garden brown out at a few stage in the summer time. This will in the end cross lower back for the duration of the wintry weather length. In leaving or not it's miles, you'll no longer best keep greater, but you'll furthermore feel a good deal plenty less pressured.

20. Get a timed sprinkler. If you truely don't need to see your garden go brown, you could get a timer for sprinkling it. This may also need to assist you avoid forgetting to expose it off.

21.Turn off the water heater after the use of it in the morning. Actually, you could turn it off after any bathe.

22. Hand wash dishes. You could see a huge drop for your electricity invoice in case you opt to manually wash dishes in location of putting them within the dish washing system.

23. Don't use disposables. If you use plates, spoons, and knives, those can be taken into consideration as little wastages that might ultimately pile up. It is higher to spend money on reusable meals utensils and plates.

24. Use your email or immediate messaging or maybe SKYPE. This ought to save extra money than having to call prolonged distance. With the improvement of era, you may honestly take benefit.

25. Invest in reasonably-priced furnishings. You can search for wonderful offers in online shops and thrift shops. Also, you shouldn't underestimate the extremely good of those devices as they are capable of show to be excellent unearths.

26. Use family photos for decoration. Although it may cost a few coins to have them published, circle of relatives pix might be splendid decorations to your own home. It can upload the homey sense internal your house and it would take numerous area.

27. Use your infant's artwork. Decorations might be more amazing within the occasion that they were made with the useful aid of your circle of relatives. An instance can be the drawings and paintings of your personal toddler.

28. Be minimalistic. This is an idea that is apparent but could show to be green.

With fewer gadgets in your property, you want much less upkeep and lots much less coins.

29. Recycle. You can reuse antique plastic containers for storage. Be modern and endure in mind techniques to make use of objects round your own home.

30. Don't upgrade appliances that still paintings. As long as you enjoy the characteristic of your private home equipment, you want to no longer fear about upgrading them. Instead, make sure that they're well-maintained at the manner to final.

31. Create a compost pit. This can be an environment great method that can reduce your rubbish payments. Also, this will enhance the soil of your heritage. You can then recall planting proper here.

32. Wash and iron your personal clothes. This may be tiring, however this can be

very rate-saving. Also, it'd assist equip you with sensible lifestyles values that you could use inside the future.

33. Have a minimalist material cloth wardrobe. You can also try and use informal pants, denims, and other smooth apparel. As strong colored clothes are less pricey, you could don't forget using the ones patterns. This may additionally purpose you much less pressure while you pick out out apparel.

34. Follow washing and drying instructions. To preserve your clothes, make sure which you take a look at the washing commands. These ought to help in retaining the superb of your clothes.

While all of the thoughts proper right here are promising, you must however be smart sufficient to choose out which to comprise to your home. Your community, region, and distinct out of doors factors are crucial on your choice of being frugal. Of route, you want to consider that frugality doesn't propose sacrificing your residing requirements. Rather, it should cause to help you beautify your scenario.

Chapter 14: Being Frugal With Transportation

Transportation is a need for lots humans. Whether you're going to art work alone or taking area a avenue revel in collectively along with your circle of relatives, you may obviously need transportation to get to your tour spot. Depending on how a long way the vacation spot is, this can be very highly-priced. Expensive trips aren't preferred even as dwelling frugal particularly if you plan to have them a couple of instances.

Knowing this, you need to recognize which you ought to plan your transportation approach cautiously. Depending in your options, transportation can fee or prevent cash. Keeping this in mind, you may begin slicing your costs with the useful resource of considering the ones following tips.

1.Find a automobile or van that may match your entire own family. If you're now not a big fan of cars, you can discover the most green car to your own family. This might probable shop extra money and you will ought to worry an awful lot much less approximately keeping this. You can surely education consultation the time table of your circle of relatives to keep gas and precious time. If you are married, you could percent the automobile together along with your associate and create a time table even as to bring the children to high school or choose out them up.

2.If feasible, get a smaller car. You can hold hundreds of bucks thru manner of going with a smaller car that would provide the identical utility to your circle of relatives. For instance, you can get a vehicle in preference to a SUV. Of path, you still need to don't forget the comfort of whomever you need to adventure the auto but the financial financial savings in gas, insurance and upkeep can be really worth the inconvenience.

3.Buy a used automobile. You don't want to shop for a brand new car. This can also take extra months to pay with all the added taxes and whatnot. Instead, you may look for a reliable secondhand car. However, you ought to make certain that you discover the proper supplier and be aware of something troubles the used car might also moreover have. It is super to invite approximately the facts of the auto and exclusive records regarding its performance and possibly view the automobile Carfax or comparable file. Also, to maximize your financial financial financial savings, you could even try to negotiate with the seller. If you're an remarkable negotiator, you can get the automobile for a lower charge!

four.Try to pay for the car coverage on an annual foundation. There are perks and reductions while you pay the ones in entire. This would be better than monthly installments. Of path, you can additionally make use of unique strategies to get those coverage perks. By being a regular driving stress, you can gift a secure the usage of record. You also can try and find out the maximum reasonable charge to your coverage. Your loyalty to a sure insurance employer also can bypass a long manner in phrases of introduced blessings and member privileges. Some groups moreover offer discounts for affiliations with AAA or through positive faculties, jobs or shops. Ask your enterprise within the occasion that they have got any specific offers for stepping into full and any discounts for affiliations.

5.Maintain the condition of your automobile. Cars can serve your family for a completely long term so long as they may be well cared for. You have to make it a factor to constantly test the tires to appearance that there's nothing wrong with them. Having them checked often might moreover be ideal to make certain that they're but inexperienced. Also, you need to have these tires well inflated. Always make sure to test those especially in case you plan to go on prolonged trips. Flat tires may be very dangerous and may positioned your family at danger for street injuries. At the same time, improperly inflated tires may additionally additionally require your automobile to apply more fuel and can also reason the tires to place on quicker. Another trouble you can do is to frequently update the air clean out of your automobile. It is pretty easy and you may do it yourself! This may want to help you maintain cash from having other human beings do that for you and it'd benefit the automobile in the long run. To make sure that your automobile moreover stays healthy, ensure to exchange its oil frequently. If you can, try to learn how to trade the oil of your very own car. Gaining data on retaining your very personal automobile won't most effective gain your pockets, however can also are available accessible at some stage in emergency situations.

6.Drive well. This can assist keep your car. This would moreover placed an awful lot a whole lot less danger to your vehicle being damaged in injuries. Also, if you accelerate, you could end up the use of greater fuel than essential. This might also positioned you at threat for pricey tickets. Hence, make certain to comply with all site visitors recommendations and be a accountable driving force.

7.Try hypermilling. Hypermilling includes clever strategies on the way to keep fuel on the equal time as you're on the road. For instance, you may turn off the engine of your automobile at the same time as organized at a prevent light. Just ensure that you have a logical foundation on why you could perform a high quality motion to save you any unwanted risks.

8.If you're worried approximately traffic, leave earlier. Sometimes, it can be very tough to awaken early in the morning to depart for paintings. However, this can spell the distinction between a 5-minute adventure time and half-hour adventure time. If you're inclined to sacrifice some precious mins of sleep for more financial savings, you then need to try this tip.

nine.Try to find out possibility routes to keep away from site visitors. You can talk over along with your map or ask your buddies about awesome procedures to get to sure locations. You don't should brave via the mayhem of internet site traffic.

10. Avoid prevent and pass traffic. This ought to use up extra gas as your vehicle

could need to again and again conquer the friction of the road. Hence, it's far higher to journey on a easy flowing avenue to avoid those undesirable wastages.

11. Use the air conditioner at the same time as crucial. Air conditioning can surely purpose your car to deplete greater gas. If you may, use it very sparingly and simplest on very warm days. If it isn't terrific-warmness outside, you could decide to show this off to shop greater fuel.

12. Make a listing of all errands and locations you want to go to. This ought to prevent pretty a while. In getting ready for the experience, you could already plan what precisely you're doing. You may be capable of formulate the path you will be taking, consequently maximizing your fuel.

13. Try to decrease grocery visits. If possible, purchase all the additives you could want in a single grocery go to. This

could help you preserve more on gasoline. A beneficial tip may want to encompass now not going to the grocery besides you have placed 10 items to your grocery listing. Also, you can create menu plans to already have an focus of what to get from the grocery.

14. Remove useless heavy devices to your automobile. The lighter the automobile is, the higher. Weight performs a position on the quantity of fuel fed on via your vehicle.

15. Shopping online can shop gas. Instead of having to exit of your house to buy topics, you could just do it on line. Of path, you want to make certain which you aren't spending greater on the gadgets which you're ordering.

16. Don't overfill the gas tank. This might also truly be inefficient due to the reality the fuel may additionally furthermore drain down the difficulty of your vehicle.

Moreover, this will damage your automobile.

17. Take phrase of your fuel mileage. Whenever you excursion, try to degree how lots gasoline you operate. If the miles in step with gallon start to decrease, you could try and see what's inflicting this problem.

18. Try to carpool with remarkable humans. If you don't want to deliver a automobile, you may attempt to look for carpool buddies interior your place. You can experience with them going to artwork or one in every of a kind places.

19. Commute. If you may't discover humans to carpool with, you could continuously try commuting. Public transportation may be less expensive than spending cash on fuel. You definitely should discover the fine route with a view to offer you maximum pleasure. Also some

employers offer a transportation plan permitting you to pay for a number of your commuting charges with pre-tax greenbacks saving you more money. For more in this observe the following records on pre-tax transportation payments determined right here http://bit.Ly/1yyP6G9.

20. Use a bike. A wholesome possibility to commuting or the usage of automobiles might be to use the old school motorcycle. Not quality would not it assist you maintain fuel, you may moreover workout and extend a extra healthy way of existence by way of manner of using a bike. This may be tiring, however it may be certainly without a doubt worth it in the end.

21. Walk. If you virtually don't need to use any shape of transportation, you may commonly motel to strolling. This could be very practical particularly in case you're

going to locations which can be as an alternative near. Walking may additionally assist you burn a few calories!

In choosing the tips to use, you want to hold in thoughts that safety and universal performance are despite the fact that your priorities in phrases of transportation. It wouldn't be logical to sacrifice the tremendous of your transportation if this can positioned your health or existence at threat. Hence, you need to maintain in thoughts all of the dangers and blessings of selecting new transportation strategies if ever you select out to apply these.

Chapter 15: Travel

At sure elements of your life, you may obviously experience tired out of your normal normal. You can come to be burned out from artwork or specific stressful conditions. This makes you recognize which you need to take a smash and bypass on excursion. Going on vacation is a high-quality way to unwind. You can spend time together together with your circle of relatives and discover locations spherical the sector. It may be fresh to carry out a bit element new for a change. Of path, those trips would possibly propose spending money.

As many holidays would require you to shell out a big quantity of economic savings, you need to don't forget the maximum efficient plans for the revel in. It continues to be feasible to adventure and revel in your self at the same time as being frugal and sensible!

1.   Plan trips in areas in which you have had been given circle of relatives and friends. If you realise humans residing in a certain area, you can try to ask them if they are able to display you spherical that place. Even higher, you may even ask in the occasion that they wouldn't mind having you live in their houses. This may want to save you pretty a few cash. Instead of having to spend for inn expenses, transportation, meals, and loads of other topics, you can live with pals or own family. Of direction, be terrific and don't abuse their kindness.

2.If you don't understand every body in the area, look for the high-quality fees. Do some studies on the vicinity. It is feasible that positive accommodations there are providing promos or earnings. This can be sensible mainly because of the fact you would need to pass there via your self or collectively along with your family. Hence, you need to be informed of all alternatives you could take in an effort to maximize your live.

three.Stay outdoor expensive towns. If you want to go to Paris or New York, you need to try to stay in areas near the stated metropolis. Staying in the city can be very pricey. On the alternative hand, going to shut with the aid of towns or cities may additionally notably reduce the rate. Even if you have to take transportation to go to the town, you'd be spending an entire lot plenty less.

four.Travel in pairs. While travelling with a companion ought to have emotional advantages, that is moreover practical. Double rooms are typically as steeply-priced as single rooms. Aside from this, you may even percentage meals along side your accomplice.

five.Travel in a hard and fast tour. These applications must encompass promos and particular reductions. Also, you wouldn't should worry about accommodations, food, and special costs as you'll definitely have to pay the excursion business employer the bundle deal charge. Everything is probably in location and you'll definitely ought to attend and revel in.

6.Drink water. If feasible, really drink the water available. However, ensure that that is steady. You wouldn't need to get danger getting unwell. That may charge you extra.

7.Airline Ticket Discounts. Look for discounts and compare offers that are supplied. These might also need to assist in spending a fantastic deal a whole lot less for the preliminary revel in preparations.

8.Connecting Flights. You can also sincerely keep extra money in case you prefer to take a connecting flight in choice to a right away one. Although this may be more tiring, it could be really in reality really worth the saved cash.

nine.Round Trip Tickets. It is viable for one way tickets to be very high-priced. Try to test your alternatives on buying round adventure tickets.

10. Consider educate excursion. Airfare can grow to be very pricey. If possible, try looking at the selection of visiting by using way of way of teach.

11. Try to adventure at night time time. If you're journeying through way of plane or train, you could recollect travelling at night time time. You is probably capable of sleep onboard as an alternative of getting to invest in lodge lodges. Though this may be physical tiring, realise that it's far viable.

12. Go on a cruise. If educate adventure isn't viable, strive thinking about cruises. These might nevertheless be a great deal much less highly-priced than aircraft rides. Also, you'll be capable of go to particular areas even as being fed a whole lot of meals.

2.Travel after the height season. Although it can be difficult to do this in case your youngsters are in college, many right gives may be determined in some unspecified time inside the destiny of the off-season. Also, it'd be a extra exciting excursion as tons less people is probably there in your dream locations.

3.Travel moderate. Aside from being extra convenient for you, this will help you avoid any greater package deal costs. As you discover the vacation spot, you'd buy souvenirs or special devices. Of direction, you would be able to have an less tough time storing these inner your bags with out exceeding the load limit even as you move back home. This might also have a observe very an entire lot to airplane trips.

4.Pay hobby for your food intake. Depending on the location you're visiting, meals may be very highly-priced or pretty reasonably-priced. Make sure to do research on this information in order to devise how masses food you want to strive out during your journey.

five.Cook for your self. Even in case you're on tour, you could strive cooking your non-public food. This can be very a laugh and exciting with the fashion of food merchandise present in your excursion spot.

6.Avoid inn breakfasts. These may be very highly-priced. Instead of availing of such breakfasts, you may go searching and look for much less steeply-priced eating locations. Or of course, you could prepare dinner dinner your very own food.

7.Eat extra throughout lunch. Lunches are usually less costly than dinners. With this, you could shop up as you pay for lunches and pay much less for dinners.

8.Pick locations in which you really need to go to. When touring, you glaringly sit up straight for seeing new subjects. Of course, by the time you arrive on the location, you'll be beaten with all of the traveler points of interest available. However, you should comprehend that going to all of those might be impractical and highly-priced. Given this situation, you need to be aware about the areas you do need to go to. You want to set your priorities and take a look at your budget.

nine.Avoid taxis. If possible, try and discover specific options or stroll for your locations. Taxis can be very pricey in overseas regions.

10. Be aware of the foreign money. You need to have an concept approximately the modern trade price for your holiday spot. This could assist you suggest your expenses higher.

eleven. Duty loose stores may be well nicely worth it. Although the ones shops won't be the best gives spherical, they'll be appropriate as they'll be tax-free.

12. Talk with the locals. These humans may be beneficial and may even display you great restaurants and sights which may be cheap. Also, it is probably quality to make new buddies.

13. Bring your identification playing cards. Attractions like museums and problem parks may additionally have discounts for college children or senior residents.

Bringing your ID might be beneficial in case the ones promos are available.

14. Try one-of-a-kind fun sports like tenting! You don't need to transport on a grand journey to a few far flung place. You can do easy sports like camping in a nearby wooded location. It may be a sparkling getaway and you'll however be capable of lighten up.

The most vital factor of touring is which will revel in and unwind. You want to make the maximum out of those journeys and produce returned super recollections as a manner to reminisce approximately. Being frugal want to now not be a trouble for your happiness within the path of these trips. There will constantly be tactics to make the experience amusing at the same time as also price-powerful. Hence, you ought to plan those trips cautiously so that you and your circle of relatives will respect them.

Chapter 16: Personal Welfare

You want to attend to yourself. With all of the pressures and stress of existence, you need to ensure that you are well and alive to carry on along with your responsibilities. Hence, you have to commonly preserve in mind your personal dreams. There are many strategies that permits you to increase your way of lifestyles and be frugal. You simply have to be open-minded and inquisitive about trying new subjects. The guidelines indexed here cause that will help you on what you could do to make the maximum from your non-public desires in normal lifestyles.

1.Take care of yourself. If you're wholesome, you wouldn't want to make commonplace visits to the medical physician. Moreover, you wouldn't need any drug treatments. This might be of superb benefit to you and your family. Be nice to exercising and devour the proper meals to improve your fitness. Furthermore, take precise care of your teeth. Cavities must be averted as the ones can result in pricey dental corrections and different procedures. If you make investments a while in your not unusual health, you could revel in the blessings ultimately. (If you battle with weight problems or more weight you can gain from some of the guidelines mentioned in my e-book 50 Quick Easy Weight Loss Tips. For extra information download your reproduction right here http://amzn.To/1PSHrI7)

2.Stop smoking. Aside from being risky for your fitness, smoking is as an alternative high priced. Each % can rate greater than $20. Knowing this, you have to avoid the addiction. Even higher, you need to in no way begin it.

three.Stop eating. Alcohol consumption can in the end produce awful results in your body. Other than that, the actual alcohol can be steeply-priced. Hence, you must recollect minimizing this workout or perhaps stopping this.

4.Drink Water. Instead of consuming sodas, juices, or special beverages, you may attempt eating water instead. This is masses less expensive and extra healthful than the alternative alternatives.

5.Eat plenty much less meat. Meat may be very high-priced. To upload to this, more disease can arise with too much meat and too few leafy greens. While this tip doesn't inspire you to come to be a vegetarian, what is essential is that you create a balanced food plan. Adding vegetables in your food is as a substitute encouraged.

6.Reduce junk meals and special comfort food. Prepared and packed meals can be very smooth to prepare dinner. However, the ones are extra steeply-priced than truely cooking the food via your self. These can also be an awful lot much less wholesome and can undergo horrific effects.

7.Eat sweets moderately. While cakes are precise, ingesting an excessive amount of of it is able to be horrible. This can increase sugar tiers in your frame and located you at threat for cavities and health troubles. Hence, you need to be privy to how lots sugar you devour.

8.Make your very personal lunch for art work. Instead of getting to devour out for lunch, you could supply your non-public lunch to paintings. Place it in a brown bag and you're properly to transport.

9.Have a weekly menu. In knowledge what to devour, you may plan the expenses you're going to have. This may additionally moreover help you show the projected strength that you'll intake.

10. Utilize leftover high-quality meals. You can opt to put together dinner dinner extra than enough food for dinner or lunch. Afterwards, you may keep the leftovers. These may be used as food for the last days. Through this method, you will be able to keep masses. First, you may need masses less power for the real cooking technique. Second, you'd need plenty much less water to clean the cooking material used. Third, you may spend lots much less time making ready meals.

eleven. Eat out less. Eating is obviously a massive a part of your life. Hence, this will certainly turn out to be high priced. To lessen charges, you could invest in mastering the way to put together dinner delicious domestic meals as an alternative of getting to buy cooked food.

12. Grow stable to devour flowers on your garden. You can plant veggies, spices and fruit timber in your once more outdoor. Once those develop, you can constantly use them to your personal recipes!

thirteen. Plants seeds. It would price lots lots much less to plant seeds than plant small timber or plant life. Consider looking on-line for charges of seeds and notice the excellent offers you may find out.

14. Exercise for your non-public. There are many wearing activities which could help maintain you wholesome. You don't continually want to visit a health club. Gyms may even fee masses due to monthly club expenses, transportation charges, and various factors. In order to satisfy your exercise wishes, you can seek on line effective sporting sports that may be finished at home.

15. Create your personal health club at your private home. You can region a weight set to your garage or basement. This is probably a valuable investment that you may use at any time.

sixteen. Go going for walks. This likely is the most inexpensive workout. Prepare your walking path, on foot shoes, and water and you'd be set!

17. Get a easy haircut. You could should spend an awful lot less time keeping your hair. This would moreover require less shampoo and water for rinsing. Also, easy hairstyles may be very lovely.

18. Cut your non-public hair. Haircuts can be very costly in recent times. If you are capable of find out a way to reduce your very own hair, you'll shop a large amount of cash ultimately. Of direction, you may ask a family member for assist.

19. Dry razor blades after shaving. You can use a towel after using it. This might be very useful in prolonging the life of your razor. Hence, you will be capable of use it multiple instances before throwing it away.

20. Look for cheaper cleaning soap and shampoo. There are many manufacturers to be had. You actually must examine expenses and notice the remarkable of those products. Just because of the truth it's far cheap, it doesn't endorse it's less effective.

21. If you do have oily pores and pores and pores and skin, use extra committed cleansing cleaning soap for your face. As your face will be sensitive, you could make investments on better cleansing soap just for your face. You can keep the utilization of diverse forms of soap in your pores and skin.

22. Minimize make-up. While you may enjoy extra confident with make-up, you could attempt the use of it a exceptional deal less. Not nice may additionally want to you've got were given a good deal much less danger of developing zits, you will spend a good deal much less for splendor merchandise.

23. Use small quantities of cologne or fragrance. You do now not must pour the actual liquids onto your body. Don't overdo those scents. Just a minimal amount may additionally need to already be enough.

24. Use a great deal much less in sizable. Whether it's far shampoo, toothpaste, or other hygienic substances, you could attempt using a good deal less. This should assist you cut charges from purchasing for quite a few these products. Of path, make certain that the smaller portions are

though substantial sufficient to satisfy their purposes.

25. Every drop counts. Aside from this utilising to water, this may additionally exercising to merchandise like shampoos. You can choose to cut the bins of these merchandise so that you can get the ones difficult to reach bits. With that, you will be able to use it all up and keep away from wastages.

It is obvious that being frugal is no excuse a good way to be plenty less healthy. By all manner, you are attempting to be frugal to maintain in your destiny and to avoid unwanted conditions. However, you'll want to help your destiny self with the aid of way of way of moreover stopping dangerous ailments or precise nuisances that might cost even more money. Hence, continuously taking note of your private welfare is vital.

Chapter 17: Frugality While Shopping

Shopping can be a extraordinary way to praise your self. After hours of running, you can exit and lighten up. In fact, many people find seeking out new matters to be very healing. However, searching for ought to usually entail one vital element: spending cash. For the frugal person, he may think that shopping for is something that shouldn't be taken into consideration. However, it's miles possible to in spite of the truth that go shopping and be frugal! In reality, here are some tips that will help you maximize your shopping experience at the same time as maintaining your frugality.

1.Buy garments at a thrift shop. If you aren't emblem-aware, you can commonly try to appearance for proper offers on the network thrift maintain. There are many clothes which is probably priced decrease than the ones decided in department shops and supermarkets.

2.Buy notable clothes. Buying cheap garments doesn't imply looking for subpar apparel. You need to ensure the splendid of those garments simply so those truely final. To look for durable clothes, try to check the sewing of the garments. Check for unfastened threads and try to gently pull it. If it isn't stitched properly, you may observe it to appearance extra fragile. On the opportunity hand, you need to additionally test the material. The styles have to healthy. This would imply that it became created nicely. Also, try to bunch it for your hand for a few seconds. After doing this, you want to look if the cloth may go back to its natural form with just a few wrinkles. Also checking freed from rate buttons might help propose the fine of the clothes.

3.Use a rewards credit rating rating card. This is ideal for people who can control their spending impulses. You can get promising bonuses from your purchases and the cash lower back capacity is exciting.

4.Use coins. Although you may typically be using your credit card for buying, you could moreover try to use coins. For a few cause, individuals who use coins may moreover end up greater privy to their prices as there can be a tangible feeling linked to maintaining real coins. On the opportunity hand, you need to be cautious as having pocket coins can also produce the opposite effectimpulse shopping for.

5.Treat yourself from time to time. You ought to at the least experience your tough earned cash through treating yourself to rewards. If you repress yourself from spending, you may finally snap and continue to overspending. Everything completed reasonably might be the right.

6.Place highly-priced purchases on hold. You can be very tempted to buy the ones designer luggage or footwear. However, hold in mind that it's possible for those to fee plenty a great deal less inside the destiny. Moreover, before looking for the ones, try to find out higher expenses on-line or at manufacturing facility stores for the fashion designer in query. Look out for profits and are looking for promos. More importantly, make certain that you have satisfied your self approximately simply searching the stated item.

7.Be honest in your buddies. If you flow on a buying spree together with your friends, you have got to tell them of your limits. Do now not supply into the strain of having to buy steeply-priced devices you received't want within the future. If your buddies understand you, they wouldn't mind putting out with you even in case you obtained't purchase as many devices as they do.

eight.Buy in bulk. This can be mainly advocated for grocery shopping. Sometimes, a advantageous product may cost a notable deal lots much less in case you buy extra quantities of it. Hence, you have to find out this feature and see if it's miles nicely worth the more fee. Also, you need to make sure that you'll be able to use the entirety you bought within the future.

nine.Take advantage of buy one get one gives. These promos can every so often pop up in retail stores and groceries. Nevertheless, those can be very low-budget specifically because of the fact that you can get of the identical product for the fee of 1.

10. Don't purchase gadgets at their complete price. There will always be earnings and markdowns. Those costly ultra-modern gadgets will in the long run decrease in rate. Never be an impulse patron. With proper area and records, you could get those elusive gadgets for a lower price on the proper time.

eleven. Buy discounted tablets. If you're feeling ill, you can attempt to get less expensive tablets. Try to look on line or technique your network drug keep.

12. Generic capsules are much less high-priced. Another preference to undergo in thoughts is shopping for general drug remedies. Although they aren't branded, they may however serve the identical capabilities and will cost masses less expensive. This might in all likelihood assist you in particular if you need the said treatment for prolonged durations of time.

13. Shop at ethnic markets. You can be surprised at how cheap the items may match for in those regions. Always maintain an open thoughts and attempt to test out the ones formerly unexplored locations.

14. Learn to haggle. Put your communication abilties to high-quality use through requesting decrease fees for gadgets you need to shop for. With a pleasant persona and proper grin, the vendor may additionally clearly agree on your concept.

15. Shop midweek. Some stores can provide decreased prices even as no man or woman is purchasing for on the middle of the week. This may be used as a bonus to get remarkable deals.

sixteen. Shop in the path of regular hours. Bakeries can start decreasing their expenses once last time nears. You can all at once go to these establishments to shop for their tons less high priced goods. This is likewise outstanding even as buying vehicles and precise huge fee tag gadgets. Stores are greater favorable to negotiation in the direction of final time.

17. Be frugal in gifting. Although giving affords is a pleasant feeling, it wouldn't be first-class to overspend for devices that could receive away. You want to don't forget having a rate variety for objects. However, you need to furthermore recognize that many notable gives can be fairly priced and low value. You can search for those treasures in bazaars, backyard profits, or other venues.

18. Place a budget for tour celebrations. Christmas, Thanksgiving, and first rate unique activities can be high-priced. Although these days do come as quick as a year, this doesn't propose you have to spend a massive sum of money for the

ones sports activities. You notwithstanding the truth that want to be practical and realistic.

19. Avoid on-line impulse buys. Shopping on-line can also additionally offer you with the faux perception that money may be without troubles spent. Because the way is straightforward, you may fall prey to this trap. Hence, you will be wiser and actually save within the actual stores than to go surfing. Other than this, buying online additionally may be unstable specifically with the upward thrust of hackers and exclusive dangerous beings.

20. Use coupons. If you occur to have bargain coupons, use them. By all way, find out a way to take gain of these freebies and purchase objects at decrease prices. Many coupons can now be located on-line and right thru your mobile cellphone. Don't leave out out on those offers.

21. Check your income receipt. Make certain you paid for the right matters. This could keep away from complications, losing time, and losing coins.

22. Black Friday. This can paintings both techniques. On one hand, it's miles feasible to get splendid discounts inside the route of this infamous holiday. However, you can need to sacrifice your health and safety to get a preserve of your preferred object. If you are uncertain of taking component at some point of this national tour, make sure to be exquisite with a few aspect selection you're making. Take phrase which you're no longer the excellent one wanting to get those reasonably-priced tv sets or kitchenware.

Shopping can be very interesting. In getting fantastic gives, you may furthermore get the devices you want. Although you are being frugal, this shouldn't get inside the way of your looking for desires. Through planning and strategic searching for, you'll be capable of get your coins's actually really worth and store the extra money stored from being frugal.

Chapter 18: Frugal Entertainment

Work may be very tiring. Once the vacations or the weekends arrive, you are likely to be organized to lighten up and unwind. It is crucial on the same time as working towards frugality to devise your amusement appropriately that allows you to maximize your monetary savings.

There are many fun sports at some stage in your unfastened time and it's miles critical with a view to maintain a balanced life to chorus from going loopy from artwork. However, a few people routinely anticipate that having amusing means spending quite a few cash. This isn't continuously the case. There are many strategies to benefit delight and amusement at the same time as now not having to spend loads of coins. Here are a few frugal hints that you can hold in mind.

1.Cut your cable. With the net presenting access to movies and tv shows, you may attempt to dispose of cable from your private home. This might charge you tons much less as you can genuinely use the internet. Also, having no cable at home can inspire you to do exceptional sports activities like speak to humans or look at books. Also packing containers just like the Roku or Apple TV can can help you get admission to your preferred shows at a fraction of the rate of cable.

2.Monitor your subscriptions. If ignored, magazine and Netflix subscriptions can begin inclusive of up. Make high quality to appearance if you're honestly gaining your cash's really worth from availing those subscriptions. If not, you can strive and reduce the ones and look for one-of-a-kind approach of enjoyment.

three.Play board video games. If you like classic video video video games, these gemstones might suggest quite a few fun! You can play this with your family or buddies. This generally wouldn't require power and may keep you pre-occupied for quite a long term. Moreover, you may assemble better relationships with special people via this form of bonding.

4.Go to the library. If you want to spend time studying novels or specific thrilling books, you could head out on your network library. First of all, you will be capable of get entry to books free of price. Second, you could experience the homey environment inside the library walls. If you don't want to go out of your house, you can also pick out to search for eBooks online. Also in a few areas, people with a library card may be a part of up without value passes to shut with the aid of museums and factors of interest at splendid times of the month. Passes are typically limited and are first come first serve. Contact your local library to look if they take part in this application.

5.Take gain of loose events. Many colleges regularly invite human beings to have a look at their loose cultural suggests or lectures about thrilling subjects. Likewise, loose suggests may moreover moreover seem to your nearby mall or Public Park. If you're actually bored, you could test the ones out. Also many banks provide unfastened get proper of entry to to museums and various factors of interest on the first Saturday of the month for clients you clearly need to reveal your economic group card. Check collectively collectively along with your close by monetary organisation to appearance in the occasion that they take part inside the museums on us software.

6.Go visit choose-your-very personal farms. This can be very exciting specifically for children. You might be capable of pick out glowing prevent end result and greens. Coincidentally, you should buy what you picked for extremely low fees or maybe freeze some of the pickings for later use.

7.Volunteer at performances, stay indicates, and video video video games. Obviously, if you assist as an usher to the ones sports, you'll be entitled to be there without cost. Although your agency won't generally will let you watch the show even as strolling, you may probably benefit perks for destiny occasions.

8.Tour community agency and factories. Surprisingly, this can be very thrilling and educational. Not most effective might also this broaden your information approximately system and era, you can furthermore observe some thing you observed in your personal commercial organisation or approach.

9.Have a laugh in public regions. Visiting the overall public seaside, the nearby park, or special similar areas would possibly produce hours of a laugh. You can go with your family or pals and start a sequence of fun sports. Soothing walks, bike rides, and picnics could all be first rate strategies to spend some time there.

10. Participate in schooling and golf equipment. You can enhance your understanding on diverse topics and make use of a while by using learning new topics. Moreover, you could socialize with people who've comparable interests like yours. These can be brilliant locations to make new buddies, have fun, and studies. All of these perks can be attained and not using a want a high-quality deal money.

11. Stay home. Instead of going out, you may recollect staying domestic. There is probably in all likelihood some issue a laugh to do interior.

12. Explore the net. With such a whole lot of exciting web net web sites like Youtube,

you could clearly find out nearly the whole thing on the net. You could be able to spend hours gaining greater records or having a laugh. Of direction, you need to be a responsible net customer.

13. Develop hobbies. There are many thrilling sports activities to do. You can attempt swimming, desk tennis, or one among a kind fun bodily pastimes with pals. You'll certainly ought to pay a minimal amount to get admission to the facilities, however this may be nicely well worth it. Aside from being capable of loosen up, this can also be a incredible shape of exercising. However, at the equal time as pursuits are amusing, you need to moreover undergo in thoughts if those are certainly realistic. For instance, when you have no way to spend masses truly to play golfing every weekend, try to find extra low priced pastimes.

In the stop, there are various ways to maintain yourself pre-occupied and entertained. You just have to use your creativity and imagination to find out the proper sports activities for you. This may be hard at the begin, however thru your persistence and determination, you will be able to alter to these activities. You may be bowled over at how a laugh and interesting those opportunity sports can be!

Chapter 19: Increase Your Income

We all need a hint extra money on occasion. Between emergencies and the always iminent present-giving season, there is continuously a purpose to want a touch more money.

Luckily, The rise of on-line freelancer markets including Upwork, Uber, and Fiverr have made it even plenty less hard for humans to perform a touch more jobs on the issue. These internet sites can help you provide your competencies which include writing, proofreading, voice over art work, discovering, facts access or many various things from the consolation of your house and gets a fee for it!

Last yr, a survey finished with the resource of the Freelancers Union concluded that over fifty 3 million Americans qualify and art work as freelancers via doing on line freelancing paintings as element time or maybe full time jobs. 14.3 million humans bear in mind themselves to be "moonlighters", meaning that they have got a day manner which could pay blessings while they art work with consulting or freelancing on the detail to boom their income every month.

It's an clean and splendid manner to usher in some more pennies.

How to Get a Freelance Job

Getting a freelance undertaking isn't as difficult as it is able to appear. However, in case you need to find out a undertaking that exceptional fits your manner of lifestyles and your passions, you need to take some precautions.

1) Have the proper body of mind.

You don't ought to have a degree in wonderful fields that lets in you to paintings in freelance. That being said, surely because of the fact you don't have a degree, doesn't suggest that you can't observe your passion. For example, let's take freelance writing, that is a big and growing trouble. When I reflect onconsideration on writing, an entire lot of considered one of a kind jobs come to thoughts:

•Blogging

•Writing internet content material

•Writing non-fiction ebooks

•Writing brief memories or novellas

•Ghostwriting

•Scriptwriting

•Songwriting

•Writing slogans

•Writing greeting card sentiments

•Editing

•Researching term papers

•Writing correspondence

And that's in fact the prevent of the iceberg. Not high-quality do the tasks variety in type, in addition they variety in problem remember. Do you bake for a residing? You can write about baking. Are you an accountant? You is probably a educate, a representative, write eBooks approximately finance, and so on. The exceptional restriction for your obligations is your imagination and your information.

One element that you do need to keep in mind is this side venture – your issue time undertaking – is some trouble that you need to like. You artwork an afternoon pastime as it may pay the bills, has benefits, and (if you're lucky) you're eager on. This aspect undertaking will provide greater earnings but it need to also provide you with happiness. You are giving up a number of your unfastened time to paintings so that you have to be happy while you do this artwork.

2) find out what you need to do and what your ardour is.

The subsequent step is to go out and discover what your passion is. Everyone has a passion of their lives. Some people definitely haven't placed out what that is virtually but. If you're the sort of individuals who haven't located that passion however, don't be troubled. In reality, you're in a brilliant spot. Think of it as a easy slate.

Take a weekend to your self, if you are capable. If you may't, spend a Sunday afternoon via your self to accumulate your thoughts and reflect on a few important statistics.

The first element which you want to do is to discover in which your values lie. When you do that, you'll be capable of get to the muse of what drives you. Make a list of values that you find out critical to living the lifestyles that you want. Don't fear about how prolonged the listing is. Do you discover thoughts to be vital? What approximately creativity? Or do you enjoy assisting human beings?

Although this may appear like an extraordinary assignment at this diploma, it's going to permit you to gain out to the proper people when searching out freelance paintings.

3) Check out the extraordinarily-present day sources.

There are many excellent net web sites that you can go to that lets in you to find out that side activity. Even in advance than you do your personal personal, inner research, cross in advance and test out a number of the ones internet sites to see what is available. My massive tips are:

•Upwork (previously known as oDesk)

•Craigslist

Beyond that, take a look at out some of the ones one-of-a-kind net web sites:

•Freelancer

•Fiverr

•Gigblasters

•Guru

•RapidWorkers

•People Per Hour

•Smashing Jobs

•Taskr

•Just Answer

•Job Boy

- Short Task

- TenBux

- Tutor

- Workhoppers

- YunoJuno

- Zeerk

four) Be affected individual and be organized.

It's not going to arise in a single day. You're going to need to be patient when it comes to getting new gigs and customers, in particular if you haven't gotten your foot within the door however. It normally takes a while to get momentum whilst you're beginning from scratch.

Keeping organized is a extraordinary thought but there are such a lot of awesome strategies to live organized, it nearly feels as beneficial as announcing

"Just do it." Just do what? So to be greater beneficial, I want to offer you a pair of various options. I live prepared with the aid of manner of using a aggregate of a virtual calendar that syncs with my cellphone and a hardcopy every day planner that sits on my desk.

I use my every day planner for duties and reminders of sports. If I have an upcoming reduce-off date or a string of small responsibilities that want to be finished, I write them down in there in order that I don't overlook about the small matters (and the huge looming topics within the future). I use my digital calendar for items that comprise others. If I actually have an occasion that I even have invited others to, I use a community Google calendar (which I've shared with them). I moreover add each year reminders like birthdays, tax dates, anniversaries, holidays, and quarterly critiques in that calendar. My mobile smartphone is synced to it so I get reminders in keeping with week earlier. This gadget works for me. If you suspect it'd offer you with the effects you need, strive it out.

5) Network and hold up with contacts.

Networking is like marketing. You want to preserve up with it in case you need it to help you together together with your facet commercial enterprise business enterprise. When you're beginning from scratch and also you're on the lookout for to gain momentum, your largest tool may be "phrase of mouth". Do you need to knit infant blankets as your facet undertaking? That's great! You must discover some conventions, workshops, or meetups. Find a knitting business enterprise. There, you can observe extra approximately your craft and you could make contacts if you want to look for clients or recommendation on a way to bypass beforehand together with your precise craft.

That being stated, now not anyone likes to network. Not only that, for individuals who haven't needed to network within the beyond, it would seem like an ominous project to begin on. If this sounds which includes you, take a look at out a number of those useful pointers to get you started out out:

•Ask the proper questions. When you're networking, you'll be terrified of not know-how what to say. That's quite everyday. If you're now not used to selling yourself, you is probably at a loss as to in which to start. There are 3 questions that you must virtually hobby on on the identical time as you are in a networking scenario:

o   What ideas are you able to get from others?

o How are you able to help different human beings?

o Who else are you in a role to speak to? Or who else will will let you increase your business enterprise?

•Reconnect with a few friends and circle of relatives members. You have already got a fan base from your beyond and cutting-edge relationships.

•Try to set up your furniture. I'm crucial, it truly works! Sometimes, how your place of business (or wherein you'll be installing vicinity save) is set up, you through twist of destiny hollow your self up in a small corner. Instead, attempt conducting out through shifting your furnishings so you'll be interacting with greater human beings. Will you be putting in store at home? Why now not try walking some different place every now and then? If you're a knitter, writer, or artist, attempt going to a café to art work at the least as quickly as every week. If it is sunny, exit to a park and work at any such benches or picnic tables. Get yourself on hand!

•Set up a "Meeting New People" fund. We don't all have the more money to visit conferences or conventions. If you write on the facet, the ones writing conventions can fee a fortune! So, why no longer preserve a jar in your kitchen in which you could drop your lose trade. Even in case you don't want to spend the coins to visit a convention, you may use this coins to take a class on your new location or buy dinner at a meetup group.

Chapter 20: Couponing one hundred and one

The term "couponing" has modified at some level within the years. As subjects are becoming extra luxurious and as we've started out out to collect more matters, the need for the usage of coupons has been increasingly more of a fashion. In reality, there are actually, four tiers of couponing from someone who on occasion clips coupons to someone who can be considered an "Extreme Couponer". Have you visible the TV indicates? Yes, that is real. Yes, you could try this too, if you have the time and choice.

Each stage of couponing has one-of-a-type tendencies and practices so as for that level of a couponer to benefit success.

Casual Clipper

Most humans is probably considered a casual clipper. This manner which you clip coupons on the identical time as you observe one that pastimes you inside the newspaper. To be taken into consideration in this category, you likely clip much less than 10 coupons for a ride to the groceries. You'll store a couple of bucks inside the way. The financial savings on this class is quite minimal but pennies fast grow into kilos!

Generic Shopper

For this magnificence (diploma II), you will want to save and purchase an average logo while confronted with the choice emblem due to the fee contrast. If you most effective purchase commonplace brands, you can truely store a massive chew of trade. I'm speakme loads of greenbacks a month for a own family of four.

The handiest trouble with this that sometimes the call emblem performs better than substantial manufacturers. During instances just like the ones, you don't end up saving the coins, particularly in case you need to buy greater of the time-honored product to equal the notable level of the name logo stuff.

Deal Shopper

I am seeing more and more humans fall beneath this class. If you want to be a deal customer, who subjects come into play:

1.   You simplest keep and buy matters which can be on sale.

2.   You use a reduction on these gadgets as nicely.

This will double your economic financial financial savings (or more) and there are lots of different varieties of monetary monetary savings with this technique as nicely. I even have visible many couponers who've short risen to this degree or rank of consumer and it has saved them masses of cash. The pleasant hassle is that every so often:

•The extraordinary deal comes with having to shop for in bulk, which gained't charge more but may be hard to store

•You need to journey to various stores so that you can get the superb deal.

•You may additionally moreover need a few issue precise that isn't always on sale. Once you get used to sale fees, it feels terrible having to buy some issue at whole price.

This technique is easy but it does take a few being used to. For instance, permit's say which you see a selected call emblem body wash on sale for $0.Ninety 9 about as soon as a month or so for approximately per week. Once you see that sample, you may start searching out coupons for that emblem. If you've got a $zero.50 cents off coupon for that product, you can purchase it for $0.49 cents! That's a much higher deal than purchasing for the usual brand!

Of path, this only simply works if you have the time and staying strength that it takes to search for the offers and search for the coupons.

Extreme Couponer

These people understand that you could use each an in-hold coupon and a manufacturer's coupon at the identical time. Did that you can do that? Well, now you do. Being able to use every of these coupons on an object that is already at a deal (allow's say a BOGO – buy one, get one sale) is first-rate, particularly if you have devices of coupons for each object.

Believe it or not, some of those excessive couponers even depart the store with more money of their wallet. Yes, that is immoderate! Sometimes, the huge problem with immoderate couponing is that people who do that allow it take over their lives. You don't must permit it take over your existence. Just stay vigilante for income and spend one afternoon clipping coupons.

All right, now allow's speak approximately some precise examples, we could?

Gather Your Supplies.

There are some superb coupon inserts that come within the paper. The maximum common ones are "Red Plum" and "Smart Source". If you don't get those in the paper (or in case you don't get the paper), you can go surfing and print right away from their internet website. I also advocate sorting out coupons.Com. If you want to look for even extra coupons check out a number of these ideas:

•Get them without delay from the severa manufacturers which you common. You can each bypass on their net internet web site or contact them to request some coupons.

•You can find out a few coupons at the packaging. Don't neglect to take a 2nd have a take a look at the label to see if there are a few coupons at the alternative side of the label.

•In your junk mail. Some excessive-price manufacturers have commenced out to ship their coupons thru the mail so check out your junk mail earlier than you dispose of them.

Keep Your Supplies Organized

Some huge time couponers advise maintaining a binder with baseball card sleeves and divider tabs. That can be one of the most prepared strategies to hold your coupons so as. You can either tab them through expiration date or through product kind.

The key to maintaining them organized is to discover the technique you'll get the most out of. You can each clip all the coupons which you get, and set up all of them – just in case you need one. You can lessen out the coupons that you satisfactory intend to apply. The final possibility is to hold all of the coupons intact at the page and record them away, cutting them out as you run throughout the ones merchandise.

I have strategies of organizing my coupons. I preserve all the coupons that I run all through and go through them each Sunday with the close by hold advertisements. I healthy up sale devices with coupons for the ones merchandise, lessen them out, and record them in my binder. When I pass grocery buying, I take out people who I intend to use and placed them in a small accordion field (made for coupons). I divide them up through the usage of the usage of hold rather than with the aid of product kind after which go to every hold and buy the products which might be on sale (and that I even have a reduction for) all in in the end.

Learn about Your Favorite Store's Coupon Policy

Not every keep has the equal sort of coupon insurance. Some coupons will will let you use manufacturer coupons similarly to maintain coupons. Some will only will permit you to use coupons on items that aren't on sale. Here is a handy list of links to common stores and their coupon regulations: http://frugalliving.About.Com/od/coupons andrebates/qt/Store-Coupon-Policies.Htm

Once You Know the Rules, Get Creative

You want to make certain no longer to abuse those tips due to the reality if you annoy the cashiers and bosses, they won't be so type to you at the same time as you stroll thru that door. Here are some smart techniques to get more coupons and get the most out of them:

•If you're travelling on a Sunday, check out the newspaper inserts from one-of-a-kind areas. They will (most in all likelihood) be brilliant and you may furthermore find out specific advertisements for first-rate stores.

•If you find out a particular set of coupons that you sincerely like, buy multiple papers so that you can get extra of that coupon. An greater paper might cost a touch you every different couple of dollars however if those coupons ought to save you more than ten greenbacks or so, I may also say that the more fee is worth it.

•Did you recognize that you could integrate a buy- one- get- one- loose sale with purchase- one- get- one- unfastened coupons too! Just make certain that your precise hold doesn't frown upon that. If you discover a store an excellent way to will will let you do that, you've certainly hit the jackpot!

•A lot of shops will be given their competitor's coupons. Just ask the cashier as they ring you up. Keep song of which stores let you know which you that their coverage is to accept any coupons.

•Coupons nonetheless work on clearance devices. Score!

•Many grocery cards will assist you to add coupons to them. This is a incredible way to keep cash on the identical time as no longer having to preserve a ton of coupons around with you. Just ensure which you keep song of the manufacturer's coupons which you located in your card so you don't by threat use the equal print coupon at some point of checkout. That can get difficult.

That being said, digital coupons are quite awesome. You can get them onto your grocery loyalty card. You may additionally even get them onto your cellular telephones. Some stores have apps that permit you to download coupons.

•One of my domestic dog peeves is that most of the coupons that you run into even as you're looking for a bargain, are for processed food. You don't see pretty some coupons for wholesome and natural components. However, there are some printable coupon internet internet web sites that specialize in meals which can be healthful for you – now not truely prepackaged meals. Check out mambosprouts.Com and betterforyou.Com/energetic-gives for some coupons on gadgets that assist you get and stay healthy.

•Check out some mommy blogs and deal/frugal blogs and be a part of them. If you discover one that you like (bonus factors within the occasion that they stay a life-style that mimics yours), they'll likely let you apprehend of a few superb offers in actual time. Check out organicdeals.Com or coupondivas.Com as a couple of examples to get you began out.